REIKI
Healing Yourself & Others
A Photo-Instructional Art Book

Written and Illustrated by Reiki Master Marsha Burack

REIKI HEALING

Celebrating the

Unification of Spirit and Matter

First printed
March1995

Manufactured in the United States of America.

Lo Ro Productions, Reiki Healing Institute, 449 Santa Fe Drive, # 303, Encinitas, CA 92024

Library of Congress Catalogue Card Number 93-091771

Reiki ~ Healing Yourself & Others, A Photo-Instructional Art Book Written and Illustrated by Reiki Master Marsha Jean Burack.
ISBN 1-880441-39-X (alk. paper)

The author would also like to thank the following for permission to reprint previously published material.

"Lord's Prayer" page 61 from *Prayers of the Cosmos: Meditations on the Aramaic Words of Jesus* by Neil Douglas-Klotz.
Copyright (c) 1990 by Neil Douglas-Klotz. Reprinted by permission of HarperCollins Publishers, Inc.

"Robe of Light Prayer" page 91, an adaptation from *It Is ALL Right* by Isabel M. Hickey. Copyright (c) 1990 by Isabel M. Hickey.
Reprinted by permission of Helen K. Hickey, New Pathways Publishers.

The paper used in this book meets the minimum requirements of the American National Standard for Informational Services
Permanence of Paper for Printed Library Materials, ANSI Z39.48-1984.

REI (ray)

Universal Life Energy
Spiritual Consciousness
All-Knowing

KI (kee)

Breath
Life Force
Vital Radiant Energy

Official Script Style (879-221 B.C.)

Running Script Style (25-220 A.D.)

Hands-On Healing Overview

Congratulations on your willingness to improve the quality of your life and the lives of others. Through Reiki hands-on healing, you will gain the experience of living life in a more loving, healing way. Reiki will help you access levels of knowingness, intimacy, and comfort, as well as special and unique abilities and feelings that you may have lost or overlooked.

With the simple yet very powerful tools of Reiki, you will begin to experience and effect changes in yourself and those around you in a practical and powerful way. This work strengthens all interconnectedness with ourselves, others, and universal mind. All you need is your desire.

Hands-on healing has been practiced throughout the history of mankind. Anthropological studies show that primitive people used hands-on healing, herbs, and their own minds through meditation, imagery, and journeying to create healing. Much of that knowledge has been lost and rediscovered over time. During the history of Western mankind, hands-on healing has taken on many aspects, from the miraculous healings of the Bible to hands-on healing being thought of as the Devil's work, along with astrology and other methods considered occult. In many other parts of the world, hands-on healing evolved into simple, effective, widely used systems (see suggested readings). Following the Industrial Revolution, the modern mind developed modern medicine, the atom bomb, the car, and the computer, and traditional ways remained in the background. With the rising costs of medical care and the increased stress of everyday life, coupled with our evolving consciousness, alternative forms of healing and new ways of thinking are again being investigated. Once more, hands-on healing may have a relevant role to play in our learning about the whole self (Spirit, mind, and body) and what this whole self can do.

Reiki is an easy and potent hands-on healing system. It is also a sophisticated initiation system that uses healing mantras — sacred sounds and symbols — to unify the whole self and thus expand one's healing powers. This book is for novices interested in exploring their potential through hands-on healing and for Reiki practitioners seeking to enlarge their knowledge and understanding of this art.

T a b l e   o f

C o n t e n t s

Dedication

The Diamond Light
Shimmering through all its facets
Reawakens the planet

Blessing all healers, in all capacities.

Acknowledgments

With deep gratitude to all those people
whose great support enabled this book,
so dear to my heart, to spring into being.
Thank you.

Dorothy Burack, editor

Milton Burack, advisor

Sara Pess, Reiki Master, editor

Rebecca Brown, Reiki Master, editor

Catherine Hansson, graphic designer

Dr. Jason Roberts, editor, tender of the hearth

Arline Wolfson, editor, graphic designer

Faith Damask, Reiki Master, editor

Mary Hart, photographer

Mandy Evans, advisor

Kate Hughson-Law, my Reiki Master

All my Students / Teachers

David Wick, layout, model

Debra Dilly, Reiki/Seichim Master, model

Bob Endo, Reiki Master, model

Barbara Joyce-Jones, Reiki Master, model

Lucy Wang, calligrapher

Rick Ribeiro, dc lithographics

Don Bennett, Color Graphics

Mike Bufalry, Color Graphics

George Waite, Color Graphics

Ewing Hughes, and the staff of Commercial Press

Foreword

Reiki is a key that opens the door to your heart and helps you heal your life. Reiki is a journey to the heart and beyond, a gateway to the healing of suffering and pain, a path of deep joy and inner peace. Reiki is a gift that allows us to connect more deeply with who we are and to share this intimate part of ourselves with others in a loving way.

Today there are many teachers. Now and again, someone comes along who stands out from the crowd, who shines like a welcome light on a dark night. Marsha Burack is such a person. She is a torch bearer with a message: "Love yourself, honor yourself; you are a magnificent being." Marsha Burack is a living example of these teachings. In her search, she broke through her holding patterns, began her own inner healing, and rediscovered her own power and greatness. As a Reiki Master/Teacher, she shares herself and her knowledge with all who ask.

Discover Reiki through Marsha's tapes and book and rediscover yourself. Allow yourself to tap into and drink from the Reiki river of love. Experience your own inner greatness and power.

Margot "Deepa" Slater
 Reiki-Seichim Master/Teacher
 N.L.P. Therapist
 Newlife Farm Retreat
 Newstead, Victoria, Australia

A Special Note to the Reader

I began teaching Reiki because I wanted to help people help themselves and others. I also wished to participate in the advanced energy work of initiations, central to teaching Reiki. To enhance my classes, I wrote about Reiki, including detailed descriptions of the Reiki hand positions, and read these to my students as they treated themselves in class. Their enthusiastic responses gave me the idea for the *Reiki ~ Healing Yourself* audio cassette. This tape helps people, with or without initiations, to let go at a deep level through the mediums of music and positive thoughts.

I began writing daily and enjoyed the process immensely. Working on the book, *Reiki ~ Healing Yourself & Others*, brought my thoughts into focus. I grew to understand the nature of the Reiki method, that the Reiki sound and symbols system generates a particular frequency that unifies the mental and physical bodies with universal life energy. I also began to know that *reiki* is something we naturally have and that this ability is expanded by the Reiki system. We also increase reiki by letting go of the way our "little" minds structure personal reality, thus entering into the subtle, healing field of universal life energy: this understanding amplifies treatments at any level of training.

Finishing this book also brought me to a new level of understanding and skill. The intention of Oriental painting, like Reiki, is to connect with the *chi* or energy of the brush or activity. I feel the book's writings and paintings combine to produce an artistic production whose format and layout radiate healing energy — *chi*, health, life force.

Reiki ~ Healing Yourself & Others contains valuable information about Reiki, your body, and how to practice the art of hands-on healing. For Reiki students, it is my wish that this book refine your knowledge and stimulate thought and discussion. For people in outlying areas and/or those who have difficulty finding a teacher, it is my hope that from the instructions of this book you will feel confident to give treatments — with or without Reiki training. Training is always encouraged. It is a paradox that at the deepest levels we know everything, and yet we learn in order to access those levels directly. I hope this book gives you as much insight and pleasure to use as it has given me to write and design. Some of my fifteen years of experiences as a hands-on healer appear in italics (pages 22-25 and 76-91). *Marsha*

The Essence of Healing with reiki

What is *reiki*? It is intangible, invisible, formless, not of the senses, a subtle field of energy, the essence of life,
  universal life energy.
We experience *reiki* by: remaining in the moment, letting go of thoughts, connecting to our breath,
  acknowledging any and all feelings, allowing ourselves to just be.
Reiki manifests in us as: health, joy, spontaneity, vitality, radiance, contentment, direct action, knowing, life.

Reiki is a meditative art. The treatment pattern is simple, yet sophisticated, for it provides a framework for the practitioner to shift into an active state of being. This state might also be described as an alpha or theta level of consciousness. Anyone can do this practice. In fact, one's meditative abilities are enhanced by the natural energetic connection that occurs between two people during treatments. In Reiki healing you do nothing and achieve everything. Reiki, like many natural healing methods, is a powerful adjunct and sometimes a viable alternative to the chemical/ surgical methods developed by the modern rational mind. Each way has its own right place and time.

Healing can be a mysterious process. Each person moves in his or her own rhythm. We want to take care to be open, to allow space for all of our successes and failures and also for the successes and failures of others. At times it may appear as if discomfort and pain are continuing in spite of all one's efforts. In these cases, perhaps some underlying healing process is going on or some deep learning is taking place, temporarily adding tension to the situation. Sometimes it may appear that all discomfort or pain is gone, completely dissolved. At other times it may feel as though we are moving ahead inch by inch, or in a long, slow series of plateaus.

All this, Life itself, is something we freely participate in — the gathering, storing, amplifying, releasing, and dispersing of life force — our very nature. Through our own great joy and awareness, effort and discipline, we open to the moment. And in that moment there is only love, power, and healing.

reiki & Reiki

The word *reiki* is a Japanese word for universal life energy. This universal life energy we all possess in full measure. It is the essence of us and of everything around us. It flows through our body and out our hands and feet, always, as long as we live. This *reiki* is the healing, life-giving energy that sustains and nourishes all living things. In some cultures it is referred to as *chi* or *prana*. We all have this universal life energy *reiki* flowing through and from us, and anyone with a true intention and desire can do healing work right now. There are many wonderful healers working with different modalities, or without any system, who know how to tap into universal source. One does not need Reiki initiations to be a healer.

Now, Reiki (which I will designate with a capital "R" for the Reiki method) is an ancient art designed to increase your healing potential through specific teachings and attunements/initiations. The Reiki Master teaches you about, and attunes you to, a particular language of sounds and symbols — a vibration and language that engage your higher mind. Through the use of sounds and symbols, hands and breath, a Reiki Master attunes you more directly to that universal mind. Your touch becomes more potent, and you become more deeply integrated in mind and body. The rainbow bridge to cosmic consciousness widens. Some of your cloudiness is removed.

The Reiki Master is believed to initiate the novice into a green healing ray of Tibet. Tibet was the home of rituals that breathed spirit into "ordinary" life. Through sacred ceremonies the lay person was introduced to different spiritual qualities of compassion, detachment, contentment, or peace and given sounds and symbols or prayers that embodied those qualities. The Reiki Master, through similar methods (although different sounds and symbols), initiates the novice into the sacred frequency of planetary healing energy and gives a method of practice (treatments).

In a First Level class, one is initiated and taught the Reiki hand positions. The student then gives treatments without conscious knowledge of the sounds and symbols. In advanced classes, the student learns the sounds and symbols and how to do absentee healing for others, as well as healing within the framework of one's own life — past and future.

Ancient language (sounds) and pictographs (symbols) are directly related to our environment and our nervous systems. Look at the pictograph for sun. It resembles our sun. Trace it slowly with your finger. Do you feel yourself radiating out like the sun?

Look at the symbol for the spiral. It describes and maps the spiraling movement of the galaxies that mirror spinning energies within our own bodies.

Reiki sounds and symbols are an original ancient language that links our body/mind with our deeper life, our very soul. The First Level Initiation tends to open up visionary qualities, helping you know your soul's true thought and purpose. The Second Level Initiation tends to open the heart, helping you feel more love and warmth, joy and contentment, and more ability to give to yourself and others. The Third Level Initiation tends to open the ability to manifest spiritual vision and live love in a practical, active way in the world. It is the energy of power and action.

The Three Levels of Reiki can be viewed as Light, Love, and Power. Apart from attunements and understanding the healing process, there is no elaborate training in Reiki as there can be in other healing methods. We are healing, as well as being healed, by living universal energy — Light, Love, and Power — AUM, the trinity — Om.

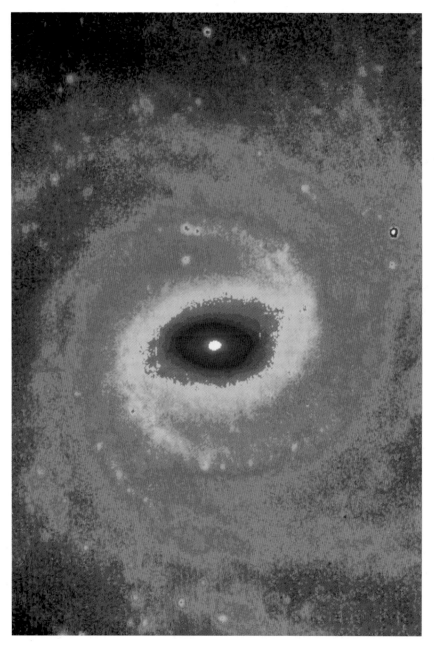

NGC 1232 Spiral Galaxy

California Association for

Research in Astronomy/ CARA

5

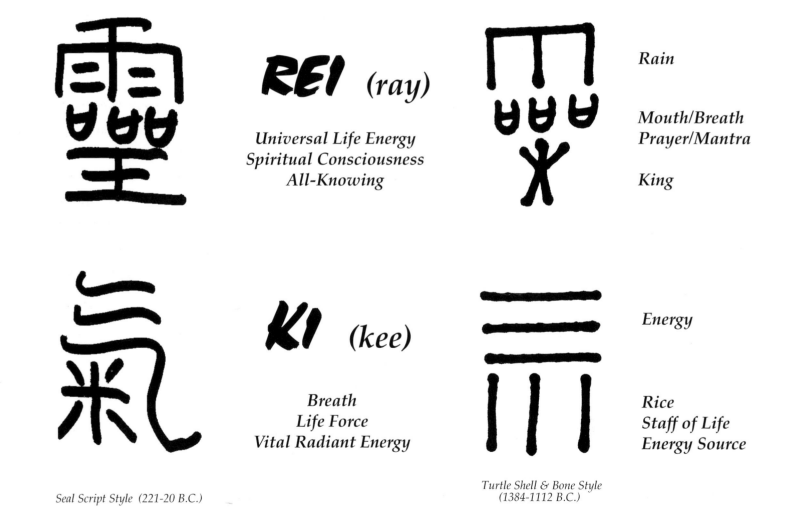

REI (ray)

Universal Life Energy
Spiritual Consciousness
All-Knowing

Rain

Mouth/Breath
Prayer/Mantra

King

KI (kee)

Breath
Life Force
Vital Radiant Energy

Energy

Rice
Staff of Life
Energy Source

Seal Script Style (221-20 B.C.)

Turtle Shell & Bone Style
(1384-1112 B.C.)

6

Reflections on the Written Origins of Rei Ki

Rei ~ the first ideograph is composed of three parts. The first means rain, that which comes from heaven and gives life to our planet. The second represents mouth/breath or prayer/mantra. With our breath and mouths we give voice to our deepest desires and truths. The third signifies king, that which rules, or the ruler or master within each of us. *Blessings from heaven, of a kingly nature, rain down upon us, responding to our word.*

Ki ~ the second ideograph has two parts. In the oldest known Chinese script, carved on turtle shell and bone, *Ki* is represented as a monolithic square or cube composed of three horizontal lines equally supported by three vertical lines. For me, this square expresses the simple, profound balance between the energies of heaven and earth, space and time, and other basic dualities. In the seal script style the top appears like a flux of energy (wave) or the ethers, the energy that surrounds us. The bottom part depicts a grain of rice. Rice is a main food supply and energy source. Rice is depicted as a cross with four lines moving toward and away from it. The horizontal line of the cross represents the horizon line of the earth, symbolizing change, giving us our sense of time, and the vertical line represents the moment, in which all space, all beingness, opens up. The cross reminds me of the very heart of matter, the heart of the moment, a space of stillness where all healing takes place. The four lines signify the four directions — north, south, east, and west — symbolizing all of creation.

Ki represents energy on the physical plane. Even before modern physics this ideograph had accurately intuited the fundamental nature of energy, which acts both as a particle and as a wave.
The energy source of divine life resides both within and without the physical form.

Reiki ~ *Heavenly blessings of an almighty power (the void, ether) rain down upon us, responding to our prayers and mantras, nourishing the seed of divine life within each of us.*

Mentally draw or image these forms and see what you experience or deeply remember (more calligraphy on page iii).

Dr. Usui, the founder of Reiki, was a minister in mid-nineteenth century Japan who wanted to know how to perform physical, emotional, mental, and spiritual healing. His search culminated in the Reiki System of Natural Healing. This is the essence of Dr. Usui's journey in poetic form. A detailed history follows.

> **He has a question, a deep burning desire.**
> **He does a seven-year intellectual search of materials.**
> **He interviews people of knowledge.**
> **He prepares himself through silence and meditation.**
> **He finds the knowledge — the keys — but not the power.**
> **He consults with another.**
> **He fasts, empties himself, and prepares to receive empowerment.**
> **He has fear before empowerment.**
> **He attains the answer: the power to heal.**
> **He needs a direction to use the power.**
> **He again meditates and consults with another.**
> **He takes action: he does healing work with the beggars.**
> **He evaluates the results: the beggars become healthy, yet don't contribute.**
> **He refines his actions: he teaches principles of living and gives treatments to those who give in return.**
> **He passes on his empowerment: he initiates others into Reiki.**

This is the path of one man's spiritual journey.
He travels from deep desire, to resolution, to contribution.
We can each be like a shining star,
Bringing a special gift to illuminate mankind.

Usui, Founder of Reiki

History of Dr. Usui

He has a question, a deep burning desire. Dr. Usui, a minister in mid-nineteenth century Japan, passionately wants to know how to perform the miraculous healings found in religious texts.

He does a seven-year intellectual search of materials. He travels to the United States (it is believed) to study at the University of Chicago, receives a degree in theology, and still he does not have his answer.

He interviews people of knowledge. He travels throughout Japan to different churches and temples, and still he does not know how to heal the physical body.

He prepares himself through silence and meditation. He joins a Zen monastery and lives a monastic life.

He finds the knowledge — the keys — but not the power. He studies the ancient Sanskrit religious texts. In these writings he finds the keys — ancient symbols and rites of empowerment.

He consults with another. He consults with the abbot about how to proceed with his search for the power of healing. Together they make a plan.

He fasts, empties himself, and prepares to receive empowerment. He travels up to a mountaintop and fasts. He gathers twenty-one rocks to mark his time and vows not to return without his answer — the power to heal.

He has fear before empowerment. On the twenty-first day he sees bubbles of light coming from afar, traveling to him with light and color and symbols. He has great fear, faints, and then wakes himself because he realizes this is the energy, the power, the transmission from the universe that he has been seeking.

He attains the answer: the power to heal. After his transmission, he travels down the mountain and is witness to four miracles. First, he has eaten no food for three weeks, and yet he has full strength to walk down the mountain. Second, he heals his injured toe. Third, he heals an innkeeper's daughter's toothache, and, fourth, he eats a full meal after a twenty-one-day fast with no difficulty.

He needs a direction to use the power. He wants a plan of action that will best use this healing power for the benefit of all.

He again meditates and consults with another. He consults with the abbot, and together they decide that it would be best to do healings on a group of people in need — the beggars. (Other versions of the story say that he went to work in the leper kingdom.)

He takes action: he does healing work with the beggars. He gives the king of the beggars all of his clothes and money, dons beggar rags, and begins to treat the beggars in exchange for food.

He evaluates the results: the beggars become healthy, yet don't contribute to society. One day he is walking on the streets of Kyoto and sees a beggar whom he treated for physical problems, now physically healthy, yet still begging. Dr. Usui then realizes that physical healing by itself is not sufficient.

He refines his actions: he teaches principles of living and gives treatments to those who give in return. Dr. Usui takes up a lighted torch and walks through the streets of Kyoto at mid-day announcing new lectures on the principles of healing. From that day on, he travels around Japan with followers, treating and teaching. All that remains of these teachings on right conduct are the precepts (see next page).

He passes on his empowerment: he initiates others into Reiki. Dr. Usui initiates Dr. Chujiro Hayashi, who opens a healing clinic in Japan. Dr. Hayashi initiates Hawayo Takata, a native of Hawaii, who brings Reiki to the mainland. Dr. Jensen (initiated by Usui) and a monk named Sagi (initiated by Hayashi) bring a slightly different form of Reiki to this country.

Love is the Great Healer

Each person is responsible for his or her own healing.
It is under his or her direction,
and you as the healer
are here to assist to the best of your abilities.

Healing can take place on many levels.
It may be an emotional healing of the heart.
It may be a physical healing of the bones or lungs.
It may be a spiritual healing of the consciousness:
the ability to embody qualities of joy, love, forgiveness
and to serve others as ourselves.

Successful healing is a matter of individual interpretation.

T h o u g h t s   o f   E a s e   a n d   J o y

Reiki Precepts

Just for today, I will let go of anger.
Just for today, I will let go of worry.
Just for today, I will count my many blessings.
Just for today, I will do my work honestly.
Just for today, I will be kind to every living creature.

Contemplate these simple thoughts.

Let go. Allow any anger or worry to surface and release.
Invite gratitude, honesty, and kindness into your life.

CHAKRAS

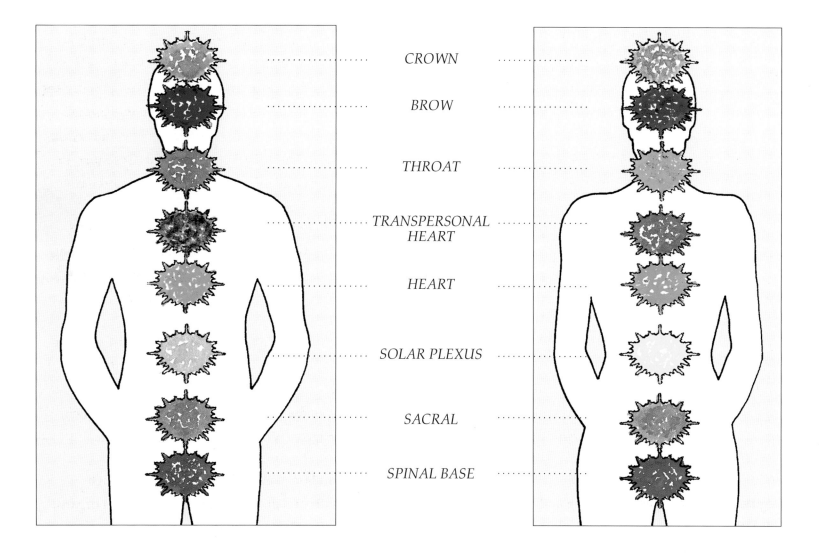

CROWN

BROW

THROAT

TRANSPERSONAL
HEART

HEART

SOLAR PLEXUS

SACRAL

SPINAL BASE

Chakras: Energy Centers of the Subtle Body

Traditional Reiki positions broadly correspond to seven major energy centers of the body called chakras, wheels of spinning energy described and mapped out thousands of years ago. There are also many other smaller centers that move and coordinate subtle energy throughout the body. The seven major chakras are often pictured like wheels or lotus flowers originating along the spine. These seven main centers start at the base of the spine with only four spokes or petals and move to the crown with a thousand petals. Each of these centers has its own color and sound, as well as powerful attributes, starting from the bottom up, of instinctual knowing, creativity and sensuality, power and action, love and forgiveness, creative self-expression, intuition, and cosmic consciousness and enlightenment. Described in recent times, the transpersonal heart (the eighth major chakra) is the center of universal love toward all mankind.

The colors of the chakras vary between systems. One chakra system might have green where another has red; this variation may describe different subtle bodies and also reflect unique emotional and mental structures found among people and cultures. The colors on the opposite page represent two possible interpretations. The texts accompanying the hand positions for healing yourself, pages 30-58, give more detailed information on the qualities of the chakras.

The ancients studied the invisible man in order to comprehend the visible one. The etheric double, an invisible form slightly larger than our body, is believed to rule the physical body. We experience this subtle body as our thoughts and feelings. Clairvoyants, people who can map these unseen worlds, tell us that chakras are etheric centers connecting the different bodies. Acupuncture and other healing systems balance subtle energy with needles, touch, or sound in order to integrate the different levels of our selves and harmonize and restore our nervous systems.

Reiki Training, through attunements, integrates our spiritual, mental, emotional, and physical bodies. Through regular Reiki treatments, we open and purify the chakras and thus revitalize related nerve plexi, glands, and organs. With the science and art of Reiki, we open ourselves even more to the divine flow of universal energy.

GLANDS

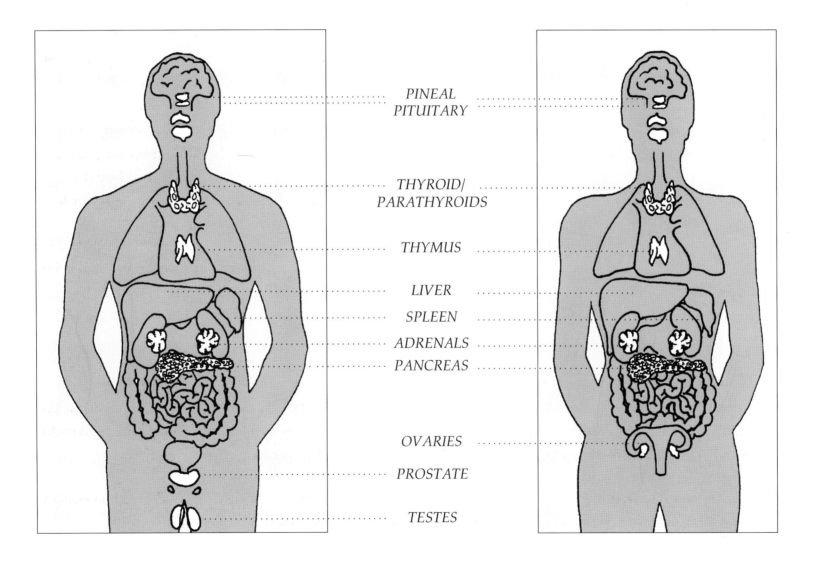

PINEAL
PITUITARY

THYROID/
PARATHYROIDS

THYMUS

LIVER
SPLEEN
ADRENALS
PANCREAS

OVARIES

PROSTATE

TESTES

Glands: Message Centers of the Body

The hand positions in Reiki also broadly correspond to the location of the major endocrine glands of the body. These regulators, weighing in at less than a pound, are of utmost importance to our well-being. They are catalysts for chemical reactions that regulate all important processes in the body — metabolism, aging, growth, stamina, weight, sexuality, moods, and the body's ability to reduce pain and heal itself. The glands work together in harmony. For example, the thyroid gland produces thyroxine, which helps activate the adrenals; the adrenals in turn energize the sexual glands, and sexual excitement stimulates the thyroid. These intricate chains of reactions are directly and adversely affected by stress. In Reiki we give an overall body treatment that reduces stress and allows the glands to rebalance body chemistry.

With the head positions, we activate the pineal gland and the master gland, the pituitary. The pineal gland, in relation to the amount of light falling upon the body, regulates skin pigmentation and sexual development. The pituitary regulates sleep, growth, and body fluids, and stores mood-enhancing hormones. Treating the pituitary enhances states of mind, heightens the senses of smell and taste, and encourages the body to replace aging cells.

At the throat position we balance the thyroid gland. This gland regulates the rate at which we burn the food we eat and the rate and intensity at which we live. The thyroid keeps iodine in the body at the correct level, at a similar ratio in our blood as it is in our mother, the sea. The thyroid gland regulates mucous membranes, aids digestion, and builds nerve and brain tissue. Proper working of the thyroid gland keeps us at the right weight for our body type.

The parathyroid glands, sitting on the thyroid, regulate the calcium in our body. The right amount of calcium enables us to feel calm and keeps our bones strong, reducing the chance of osteoporosis.

At the chest position we harmonize the thymus gland. The thymus is responsible for producing T-cells, one of the body's primary defenses against disease. This important gland is very responsive to our state of mind and can instantly correct imbalances in energy flow.

At the solar plexus (two inches above the waist), we treat the liver, pancreas, and spleen, and, with the back position, the adrenals. The liver, a major organ, metabolizes different foods, stores important vitamins and minerals, and detoxifies external and internal poisons from the body. The bile produced by the liver assists in fat digestion and keeps the colon lubricated.

The pancreas controls carbohydrate metabolism and produces enzymes that promote good digestion. Throughout the pancreas are scattered the Isles of Langerhans. These little glands regulate the amount of sugar in the blood. Keeping blood sugar balanced helps us avoid diabetes, hypoglycemia, and mood swings.

The spleen boosts our immune system by cleansing the blood of micro-organisms, producing white blood cells, and storing blood for use in emergencies. Hormones from the adrenals provide the base for the digestive enzymes and help the body fight infections, heal inflammations, and reduce pain. Proper functioning of the adrenals stimulates sexuality and creativity. Consistently balancing the adrenal glands with Reiki treatments provides quick energy, stamina, and good muscle tone.

At the sacral chakra we treat the sexual glands — the ovaries and testes. These glands regulate male and female sexual characteristics, fertility, and emotional states. When sexual energy flows through the whole body, we feel alive and happy. When these hormones are out of balance, we may experience premenstrual syndrome (PMS), ovarian cysts, or prostate problems.

This information is given in some detail in order to help us remember how much we can help ourselves when we use our hands to relax and harmonize each one of these tiny glands!

REIKI-

Healing
Yourself

Connect with Your Inner Radiance

20

You, the Healer

You *will be your own special healer, your own particular ray of healing light.*

You may be quiet, have no ideas, and reside in a deep pool of feelings.

You may live different spiritual qualities: qualities of light, love, and peace.

You may have experiences very different from our rational workaday world: unfamiliar sensations in your body, colors in your mind. Manifestations from other worlds may appear, carrying different gifts.

You may develop intuitions that guide you to move your hands to a particular area on the body.

You may develop psychic abilities:
> *~ the ability to see into the body*
> *~ the ability to describe and move patterns of energy*
> *~ the ability to know emotional or mental patterns related to an area of tension (for example, you sense that*
>   *your client contracts his shoulders due to a need to be perfect).*

Special abilities are wonderful and exciting. Nevertheless, you do not need them to do great healing work. Relax and simply work the way you do.   **Just be.**

Healing Yourself

Be Your Own Best Friend: Treat Yourself

Doing healing work on yourself, you become your own therapist, your own best friend. Sometimes you feel wonderful and your treatment is harmonious, even better than when other people have treated you. Your breath deepens; you feel uplifted. Sometimes you do not feel as good, and it may seem as if you have lost the *reiki*. You might have feelings of fear, tension, anger, or restlessness at the start of each of the hand positions, or at other times during the treatment. This may be an important time for you. Perhaps a shadow side of yourself, something that is difficult, or simply something new, is appearing in the mirror of your consciousness for review and acknowledgment. Even if you are feeling tense or blocked in the moment, as long as you are letting go of thoughts and directly experiencing your feelings, your treatment is effective. Your blocks are simply appearing for release.

Give yourself full permission to stop treating yourself if it is too difficult, or doesn't feel right, and allow a few days for integration. As you continue working on yourself regularly, loving yourself, noting your thoughts, and experiencing your body sensations — pleasant and otherwise — you will find out much about yourself, and your body/mind will begin to settle. Allowing all shadow thoughts to be present as you work with your healing energy allows for deep transformation. Increasingly you will simply experience the fullness of the radiant healing energy of *reiki*.

For the first few years of treating myself, I felt uncomfortable at the beginning of some treatments as fears and anxieties in my mind arose, or my body simply seemed to become more tense for no obvious reason. Gradually as I persisted, these tensions lifted and my treatments became a constant source of strength and renewal. I had become friends with myself at a deep level.

Reiki self-treatments help heal physical, emotional, and spiritual dis-ease. Reiki helps you to experience self-love directly. It is a valuable resource that encourages you to develop a loving relationship with yourself and others and begin to take those small steps toward complete individuation of the self.

Use These Treatment Patterns for Healing

The treatments suggested in this book begin either with the head (Head Flow Treatment on page 28) or with the stomach (Stomach Flow Treatment on page 62) and continue through the body, balancing the chakra and endocrine systems. When we begin treatments starting with the head positions, we emphasize centers of universal knowledge. For many westerners the mind is tense and restricts the energy of the entire system. Therefore, by releasing mental tensions first, the body relaxes. Beginning with the head, we immediately release tensions held in the eyes, built up from what we have seen and felt throughout the day. We balance the right and left brain and correspondingly the left and right sides of the body, and we soothe the primitive brain, the home of our instinctual fight-or-flight responses.

When we begin with the Stomach Flow, we emphasize centers of feeling, action, and power. For many westerners, digestion and assimilation are poor, leading to allergies and ill health. Starting with the stomach, we heal the digestive organs and instinctive centers, allowing us to experience deep feelings of emotional warmth and well-being. Let your hands travel to different parts of the abdomen, or do the stomach flow delineated in this book. Experiment with both treatment patterns.

If you do not have enough time to do a whole flow, partial or intuitive treatments are fine. A partial treatment begins at the head and ends at the heart, or originates at the stomach and moves up to the heart, and continues to the particular area that needs attention. In an emergency, it is okay to put your hands directly on the troubled area or areas, although it is usually best to do an overall treatment until you have training in handling specific problems (see reading list).

Reiki can be done anywhere on the body. You can add upper arms, elbows, hands, thighs, knees, calves, ankles, or feet to both of these traditional treatment patterns. For those who wish to learn more about the laying on of hands and different flow patterns and methods of self-help, a suggested reading list is included on pages 140-143.

Treatment Times

There is really no formula for when to give yourself a Reiki treatment. Choose whatever time is best for you. You can treat yourself after work, before or after a meal, upon waking, or before sleep. You may want to treat yourself at night, during the day, or in the morning. Treating before going to sleep gives one a more restful night by releasing the accumulated stress of the day. Many people, without any training, naturally help themselves by placing their hands on their chests or their stomachs while sleeping. *I like to give myself a treatment when I wake up in the morning. Starting the day with a full Reiki treatment helps me feel relaxed, centered, and clear for the day.*

A full treatment takes about an hour for the front and back sides of the body. Each hand position is held for about five minutes. A short treatment takes half an hour for the front of the body plus a few minutes for the spinal release flow (see page 49). For a partial treatment, do fifteen minutes for the head down to the heart or the stomach area up to the heart, then move to a particular spot that needs more attention. In Reiki, time is our valuable resource. After a full or short body treatment, you may place your hands on a problem area for up to one hour or more. *For a period of time my knee dislocated easily. I placed my hands one hour a day on my knee, after a short body treatment. Within ten days I heard it crack, and it never dislocated again.* When you work intensively, proceed with care. Discontinue if it doesn't feel right. Remember, your body/mind is unique, and your experiences in healing will also be unique. If you fall asleep during a treatment, consider it complete: that was what was needed. If you are on a schedule, set an alarm before treating.

Treatments Are a Treat

Become as comfortable as possible. Lie down or sit in a comfortable chair. You may also treat yourself in bed. If your arms feel strained while doing the head positions, you might need to prop your arms up with a pillow. Please do not do a position if it hurts or strains you; just move on to the next one. It is okay to skip a difficult position. At each point, the energy is specific and potent; nevertheless, from any position, energy flows throughout the whole body. At the beginning of a treatment, take a few relaxed, slow breaths. As you treat yourself, your breath naturally deepens.

Treat Anywhere, in Silence or with Music

If you do decide to use music, choose music that feels the best for you. I have a student who treats himself while playing his favorite music. He says that he hears his music "as never before." *I like to give treatments to myself in silence so I can listen to the quiet and observe the chatter of my mind/body as it settles into quiet radiant energy. Often an important idea or event that I had forgotten appears in my mind, or questions that were unresolved are clearly answered.* Students who use the *Reiki ~ Healing Yourself* audio cassettes regularly tell me that the music and words of the tape are deeply relaxing and uplifting. I also have students who treat themselves successfully and happily in front of the TV. The environment that you create to treat yourself successfully is a highly individual preference. The key is your enjoyment.

Experience *reiki* and a Reiki Class

Reiki can be used anywhere, by anybody, at any time. For fun, watch how people intuitively use their hands to help themselves. One of my students told me she instinctively puts her hands on her stomach to calm her own feelings when dealing with an irate customer at work. All you need to help yourself is your own hands and body.

~ For more experience with hands-on healing, have someone else give you a treatment.
   ~ Expand yourself even more. Enroll in a Reiki class with a Reiki Master.
      ~ In class, receive Reiki initiations that make you and your healing touch more powerful. Learn more
         about natural healing and treating yourself and others.

Reiki and Your Health Care Program

Do not use this book as a substitute for medical care. These treatments treat the whole body and enhance the body's natural ability to heal itself, rather than addressing specific symptoms. Use these treatments daily to reduce stress and increase your sense of well-being. Consider these treatments a positive adjunct to your health care program.

The Basics

When you give yourself a full hands-on body treatment, your hands rest lightly on yourself. The following pages give precise directions for the Reiki hand placements. Always do the hand placement that feels comfortable to you at that time. There is usually one major position described and one or more alternatives. Each alternative has a special application.

Hands resting side by side treat the central part of the body.
Hands resting on each side of the body, fingertips touching, treat the sides and center of the body.
Hands placed left over right intensify the energy. Hands placed right over left disperse it.
Fingers together produce a stronger energy. Fingers apart create a softer and gentler energy.

Let intuition be your guide. Leave your hands in a position for as long as you want. People new to treating tend to hurry, so get a sense of "Reiki time" by timing your initial treatments to five minutes for each position. Later on, you might want to spend more time on the initial positions of the head or stomach and occasionally, there will be a spot on the head or body that feels good or you know needs more attention, and you decide to stay there longer.

Don't be concerned if you do not see the colors of the chakras. You do not need to see any colors to make effective changes in yourself and others. We experience our subtle bodies as thoughts, feelings, and intuitions as well as colors.

When you treat: do no-thing. This no-thing, however, is not daydreaming or thinking; rather it is a state of letting go, allowing all thoughts to come and go like clouds in a blue sky. The only thing you can do "incorrectly" is to think or worry while treating. Relax, and enter into this allowing, healing state of mind. At the beginning you might feel restless or tense as blocked areas, physical or emotional, come to the surface for release. If you gently persist, taking time to integrate if need be, you will eventually experience the healing energy of your natural radiant self.

What follow are verbatim texts (in bold italics) of the audio tape *Reiki ~ Healing Yourself* with detailed instructions on the Reiki hand placements. The words and music of the tape time your treatment, create a state of deep relaxation, and reprogram your mind with the following affirmations. Consider these texts as poetic, inspirational prayers. While reading the following texts silently to yourself or out loud, you might want to place your hands in the hand positions.

1. *Brow Chakra* p. 30

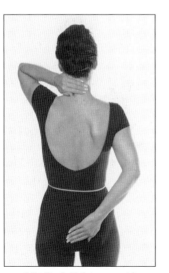

2. *Crown Chakra* p. 32

3. *Base Brain* p. 34

4. *Throat Chakra* p. 36

9. *Base Chakra* p. 46

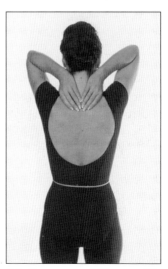

10. *Back Release* p. 48

11. *Transpersonal Heart* p. 50

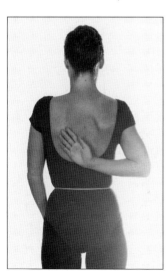

12. *Heart Chakra* p. 52

5. *Transpersonal Heart   p. 38*

6. *Heart Chakra   p. 40*

7. *Solar Plexus Chakra   p. 42*

8. *Sacral Chakra   p. 44*

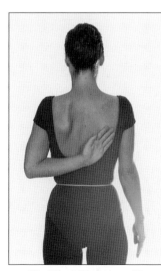

13. *Heart Chakra   p. 52*

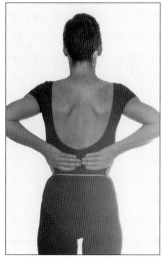

14. *Solar Plexus   p. 54*

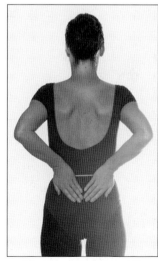

15. *Sacral Chakra   p. 56*

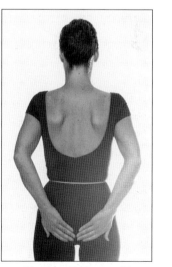

16. *Base Chakra   p. 58*

First Position: The Brow Chakra

Cup your hands over your eyes. The base of your palms will be resting on your cheekbones so that fingers point straight up. As an alternative, cup your hands over your eyes with fingers slanting slightly inward and crossing right over left or left over right, directly over the middle of your forehead and the space between your eyebrows, the third eye. Your eyes will be in darkness.

Your eyes are the gateway to your soul. The light from you shines out to others, and the light of the world shines into you through your eyes. The brow chakra, which sits between the eyes, distributes this light throughout your whole body. This third eye is the clairvoyant eye — that which can see beyond physical and intellectual knowing. It is the home of our intuitions, our inspirations.

The pituitary gland sits between the eyes, back in the middle of the head. This important gland governs the development and regulation of fluids in the body. It is the growth gland.

Relaxing the eyes relaxes the whole body. Decisions we have made about what we have seen are released, and we are able to gain a new perspective. This is one of the most important positions for the whole body and is often held for a longer time.

Indigo, a dark blue, is the color of this chakra. This color combines all colors and, like the light, is broken down into different colors and distributed throughout the whole body.

Second Position: The Crown Chakra

Place your hands on both sides of your head, just above your ears. Your fingers will meet over the top center of your head, the crown chakra. Your fingers may be apart or closed. Do what feels best to you each time.

This position opens up the seat of the crown chakra and is associated with the pineal gland. This tiny gland sits in the middle of your head. In the East it is believed to stimulate higher development. The crown chakra is our connection to cosmic consciousness. Cosmic consciousness allows "All" to enter, to enable us to become at-one-ment.

Hands on both sides of the head balance the right and left brain and, correspondingly, the left and right sides of the body. Right and left balances intellectual and intuitive minds, masculine and feminine, active and passive, and other basic dualities. Imagine the energy of these sides of your body blending! This balance brings true clarity of thought. This position treats worry, hysteria, memory, shock, depression, and motion sickness.

The color of the chakra is purple, combining the base color red and the expressive color blue. If it is a pale purple, we have full integration.

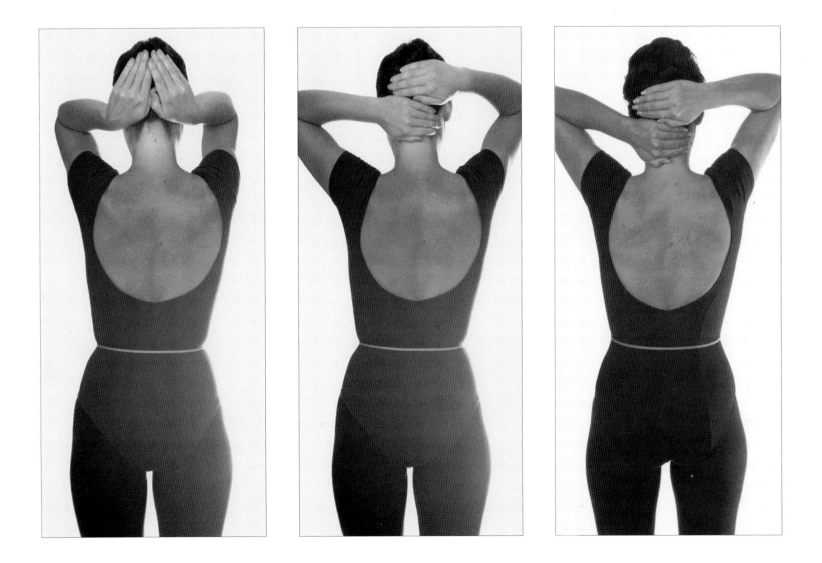

Third Position: The Base Brain

Place your hands on the back of your head behind your ears. The palm and the thumb side of your hand rest where the neck and the head join. Your fingers are placed together or slightly apart, reaching upward and slightly inward with thumbs touching. As an alternative, place your hands side by side horizontally, one above the other covering the lower part of the back of your head. Another alternative is to place your hands side by side horizontally, one hand covering the lower part of your head and one on the neck.

This position is very soothing. We are relaxing the brain stem and cerebellum, ancient parts of ourselves — the home of our universal mind. Treating this position, we act from storehouses of knowledge and power. Relaxing this area, we promote deep peace, serenity, and balance. This position helps with past life recall, insomnia, worry, and motor coordination.

Fourth Position: The Throat Chakra

Place your left or right hand around your lower throat over your collarbones, with fingers on one side, thumb on the other. Then overlap the other hand one above the other, again with fingers to one side, thumb to the other. As an alternative, place the base of the palms of both hands in the center of your throat with fingers and thumbs turned outward to the sides.

Relaxing the throat is essential and instrumental in releasing more breath and more energy to the whole body. The thyroid gland, sitting underneath this point, regulates metabolism and balances blood pressure. Imagine it glowing beneath your hands! The thyroid gland cleanses the lymphatic system, aids circulation, and prevents strokes. The color of the throat chakra is blue, symbolizing reflection, self-expression, and self-examination. "I am worthy. I have great value."

Opening this chakra reduces worry and brings energy, self-acceptance, and clarity. Blue also is the color of willpower and volition, balancing the little "I" with the transcendental "other."

Fifth Position: The Transpersonal Heart

Place your hands on the left and right sides of your upper chest with fingers slanting slightly upward, meeting in the center of your upper chest just below your collarbones. As an alternative, cross your hands left over right or right over left over the center of your upper chest. You may also place your hands side by side horizontally, one hand above the other just below your collarbones.

This position is the transpersonal heart . . . that, within each of us, which gives out instead of taking in. The transpersonal heart opens us to impersonal love and to unconditional understanding. The thymus gland sits in the upper chest underneath our hands. This important gland regulates our immune system. Opening to love and understanding, we strengthen the heart, stimulate the immune system, and protect ourselves from any and all disease. Love does make us strong! Relaxing and energizing this point, we strengthen our heart, lungs, lymph system, and circulation.

The transpersonal heart is colored pink or forest green for universal love and understanding.

Sixth Position: The Heart Chakra

Place your hands on either side of your body over your breasts with fingers meeting in the center of your chest. As an alternative, cross your hands right over left or left over right in the center of your chest. You may also place your hands side by side horizontally, one hand above the other between your breasts. This is an important position. Many people have health challenges in the breast/heart area.

This is the traditional heart chakra. This is also a seat of our emotional consciousness. Releasing this point, we open to love, peace, and contentment. An open heart is transformational, for it enables us to resolve conflicts through awareness, compassion, and empathy. Our emotions are purified in the flame of our heart.

Relaxing this point strengthens our breathing and revitalizes our lungs and heart, digestion and stomach, liver and spleen. We cleanse and relax our breasts.

Green is the color of the heart chakra, signifying good humor and prosperity, balance, and healing.

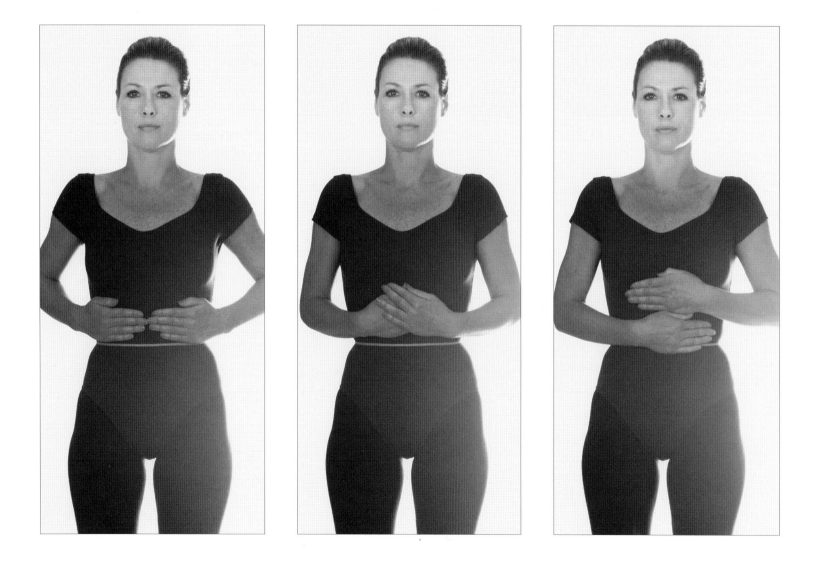

Seventh Position: The Solar Plexus Chakra

Place your hands on either side of your body an inch or two above your navel. Your fingers meet in the center of your body between your lower ribs. As an alternative, cross your hands right over left or left over right. You may also place your hands side by side horizontally, one hand above the other in the middle of your lower rib cage.

This is the home of the solar plexus. This is a position of great and immense vitality. Solar means sun. The sun is the source of our life force. Opening this point, we choose to radiate love and support to ourselves and to others in a steady, balanced, and life-enhancing manner.

Releasing the solar plexus calms our emotions and digestion. We treat our liver, gall bladder, stomach, and spleen. Releasing the seat of hurt and fear, we breathe in love, happiness, faith, and contentment. We open to correct action and to right knowledge.

The color of the chakra is yellow, signifying knowledge, energy, and power.

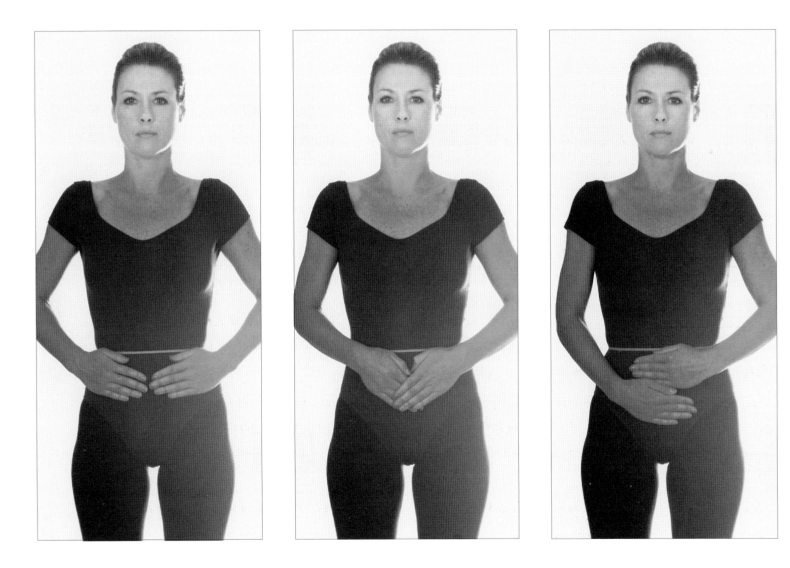

Eighth Position: The Sacral Chakra

Place your right and left hands on each side of your body, approximately an inch or so below your navel, with fingers meeting in the center of your lower abdomen. As an alternative, cross your hands left over right or right over left an inch or so below your navel. You may also place your hands side by side horizontally, one hand above the other in the center of your abdomen.

This energy wheel of creativity and sexuality is often called the sacral chakra and is the backup for the base chakra. This chakra circulates energy throughout the whole body. Opening this point, nourishing energy flows throughout our whole body.

Our will to feel, and the deep inner knowing of our body/mind, center at this point. It is the traditional point for the Zen knowing mind. Relaxing this area, we allow for a warm, feeling acceptance of life to flow. This point strengthens and relaxes our digestion, our intestines, and our reproductive organs and balances the hips, kidneys, and bladder.

This chakra is colored orange, taking us back to the happy, lively understanding and movement of our inner child.

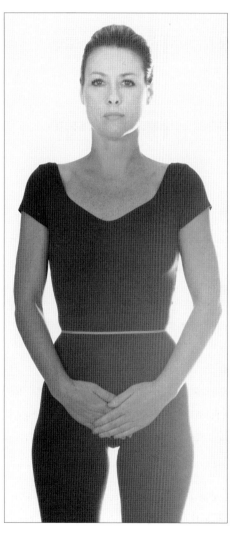
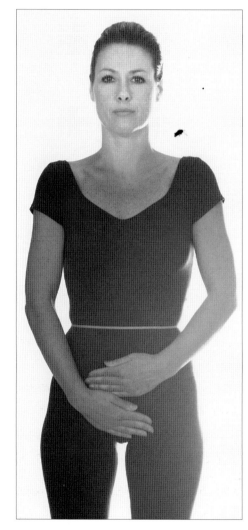

Ninth Position: The Base Chakra

Place your hands where the thigh joins the torso, fingers not meeting, hands covering where the thigh joins the torso. You may also cross your hands right over left or left over right over your pubic bone. Or you may place your hands side by side, one hand above the other over the lower abdomen and pubic bone.

The base chakra governs our basic instinct, our will to survive, to exist. This chakra rules the kidneys and supports the adrenals, gonads, and sexual reproduction. Opening this chakra brings deep feelings of peace and security. It clarifies our needs and desires and encourages us to stand on our own two feet. Knowing our bodies' appetites as well as our minds' desires, we become deeply intimate with ourselves.

The color orange/red is life-promoting — combining orange, the color of our feeling, with red, the color of fire — instant action. Orange/red puts our clarified thoughts and feelings into true action through all the chakras.

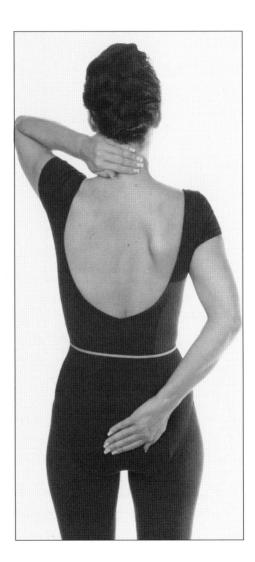

Simplified Back Treatment and Spinal Release

The following pages explain how to treat the back. If you have difficulty comfortably reaching the positions in the back, the treatment can be administered from the front. Place your hands in the front starting at the upper chest (which corresponds to the upper back) and move down the front to the heart, solar plexus, and tan tien (two inches below the waist), ending at the pubic bone. Use one of the several hand positions described in the previous sections. As a variation and shortcut for the back, you may also place your left hand on the back of your neck and your right hand at the base of your spine.

Experience the energy from your hands in the front, traveling deep into the areas in your back. You may feel the energy traveling up, down, and around your spine, releasing, relaxing, and giving breath to your entire nervous system. Breathe easily and deeply. Hold this position for as long as you like.

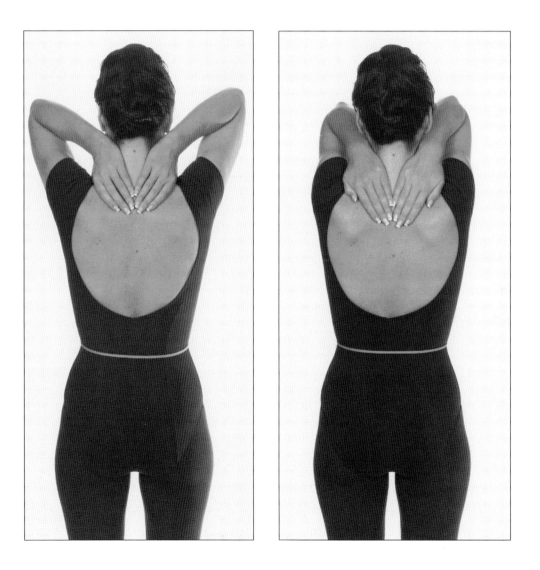

Tenth Position: The Transpersonal Heart

Place your hands on the back shoulders near your neck, with your right hand on your right shoulder and left hand on your left shoulder, fingers pointing downward and slightly inward toward the spine. Thumbs may be placed on the front of the torso or parallel to the fingers on the back. Do what feels best to you.

Relaxing the shoulders, we let go of excess baggage and allow ourselves to just be. I carry only joy! I joyfully create a new and wonderful day! Relaxing the shoulders relaxes the spinal cord, neck, and nervous system. We improve our digestion and breathing. Releasing our shoulders helps asthma, allergies, and any unnecessary weight changes. Softening our shoulders, we better access thoughts that unite all of us in love and in peace.

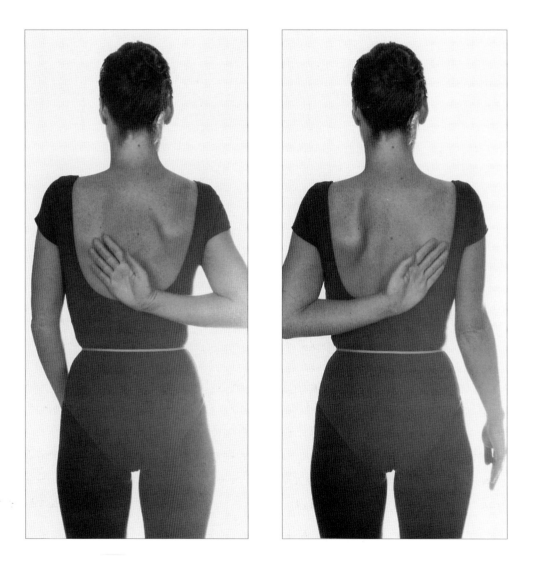

Eleventh Position: The Heart Chakra

You may have to sit up to do this next position. Please don't do this position if it is a strain. Place your right hand behind your back with palm against or away from your left upper-middle back. Treat for two or three minutes, then place your left hand on the right upper-middle back. As an alternative (not illustrated), leave your left hand in position on your right upper back. Lift your right arm over your right shoulder and place it also on your right upper back. Fingers of both your hands may meet or not. Treat for a few minutes, then do the opposite side.

Releasing these points opens us to love, compassion, and ease. We ease our breathing — our ability to take in prana, universal life force. We ease our digestion, our ability to nourish ourselves. Relaxing this area helps with constipation, fat digestion, infections, sore throats, and anemia. The heart is strengthened.

I love and accept myself! I am love!

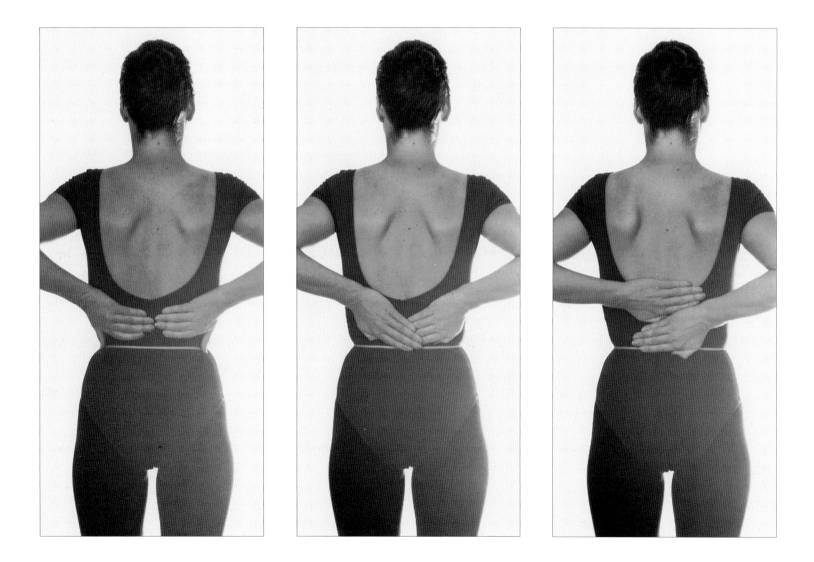

Twelfth Position: The Solar Plexus Chakra

Place your hands horizontally on each side of the back of your body above your waist, with fingers meeting in the middle of your back at the spine. Thumbs are pointed toward the waist or placed alongside the other fingers. As an alternative, cross your hands one on top of the other, or place your hands side by side on your back above the waist.

Releasing this point, we open to right action. We know what is correct. Our adrenals energize under our hands. The adrenals balance minerals, water, and proteins. Treating the adrenals, we release more energy and vitality throughout the body. We develop great stamina and improve our sex lives. This position helps hypoglycemia, fatigue, allergies, asthma, infections, and any emotional trauma.

The middle back is the support of our life. We release the middle back and let go of the past! We move forward to a bright new day!

All of my needs are wonderfully met, right here and right now! I can take care of myself at all times! I love and accept myself!

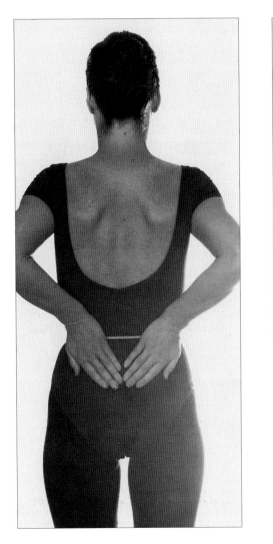
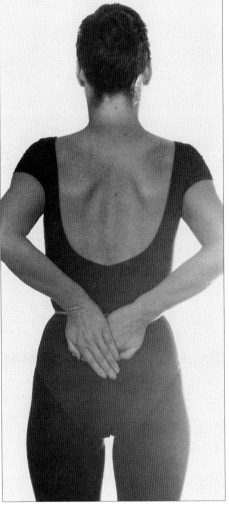
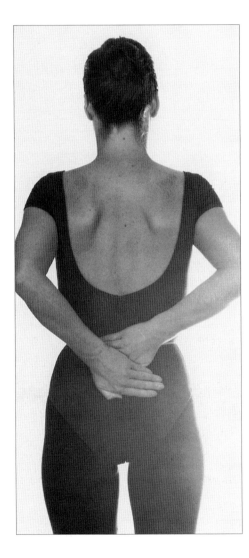

Thirteenth Position: The Sacral Chakra

Place your hands on each side of your back below the waist with fingers slanted slightly downward, meeting over your spine at the middle-lower back. As an alternative, cross your hands right over left or left over right, or place them side by side one hand above the other at the middle-lower back over your spine.

This position relates to the sacral chakra — the wheel of creativity and sexuality. Opening this area, we become alive, creative beings free to use our talents to help ourselves and others. All the abundance of the universe is available to us at this time! I am secure! All of my needs are being met!

This position successfully treats the kidneys, intestines, and reproductive system. Balancing our hips, we allow for free and easy movement throughout the space of our life.

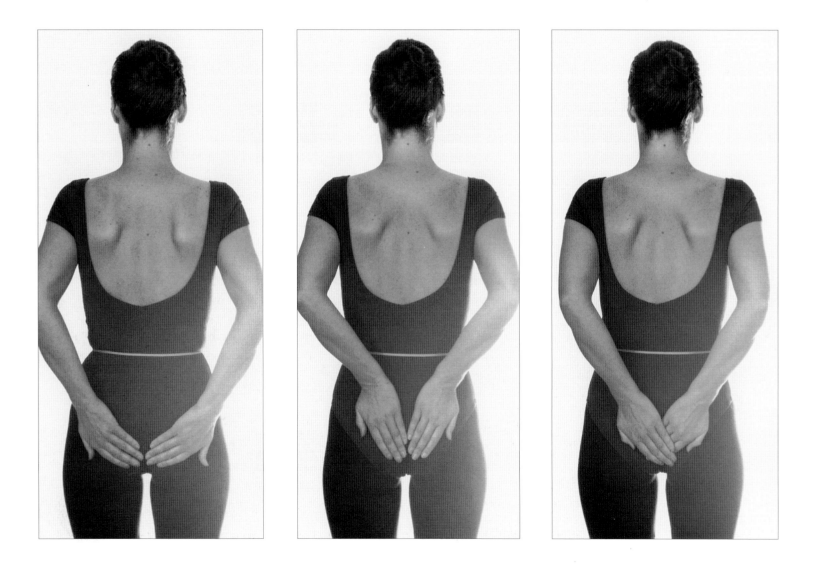

Fourteenth Position: The Base Chakra

Place your hands on either side of your lower back with fingers meeting at the coccyx, or place your hands lower on either side of your body covering your buttocks, fingers touching at the base of the spine. As an alternative, cross your hands right over left or left over right over your coccyx — the tiny bones at the base of your spine.

Treating the base of the spine, we imagine energy circulating around and through the entire spine, releasing and balancing each vertebra. We feel the energy traveling up the entire body, energizing and harmonizing the nervous system and body/mind.

Treating the hips at a deep level, we release the rectum and sexual areas, deep hidden dark recesses of ourselves.

I am secure in the deepest part of my being! I know myself! Light and love move throughout my whole being!

	The King James Version	*Adapted from* **Prayers of the Cosmos**
	(out of the Original Tongues)	*(from the Aramaic, by Neil Douglas-Klotz)*
eyes	Our Father which art in heaven	O Birther! Father-Mother of the Cosmos,
crown	Hallowed be Thy name.	Focus your light within us — make it useful:
	Thy kingdom come.	Create your reign of unity now —
back head	Thy will be done,	Your one desire then acts with ours,
	As in heaven, so in earth.	as in all light, so in all forms.
throat	Give us this day our daily bread.	Grant what we need each day, in bread and insight.
upper heart	And forgive us our trespasses;	Loose the cords of mistakes binding us,
lower heart	As we forgive those	as we release the strands
	Who trespass against us.	we hold of others' guilt.
solar plexus	Lead us not into temptation;	Don't let surface things delude us,
	But deliver us from evil.	But free us from what holds us back.
abdomen	For Thine is the kingdom,	From you is born all ruling will,
	And the power,	the power and the life to do,
	And the glory,	the song that beautifies all,
groin	Forever:	from age to age it renews.
	Amen.	Truly — power to these statements —
		may they be the ground from which all
		my actions grow: *Amen.*

Photo-Instructions for the Stomach Flow Treatment

The Home of Your Smiling Buddha Belly

The Stomach Flow Pattern begins with one hand above the waist and one hand below the waist. The hands are placed around the abdomen in a clockwise fashion, stimulating the internal organs of reproduction, digestion, and elimination — the ovaries and testes, and the stomach, pancreas, colon, bladder, small intestines, liver, and gall bladder. The hands then move to the positions for the head — the eyes, crown, base brain, and throat — and then the heart. End with the simplified back release or continue with all the back positions. For more detailed descriptions of all the alternate positions for the back, turn to the Head Flow Body Treatment on pages 51-59.

Do not hold a position if it is a strain. Experiment with propping your arms up with pillows, or whatever you can do at each position that will create comfort. For example, if your shoulders tighten in position number three, you may place your right hand on that position and rest your other hand on your right hand and/or wrist. The Reiki points are as big as saucers (six inches across) and therefore easy to locate. Let comfort and enjoyment be your guide.

Opening up the stomach area in detail promotes good digestion and elimination, two of the cornerstones of good health. Feel the release of the cooler energy from the head flow down and swirl around the abdomen, enlivening the already open and receptive internal organs of digestion, fire, and heat. Experience the comfort, knowingness, and ease of a warm, relaxed abdomen.

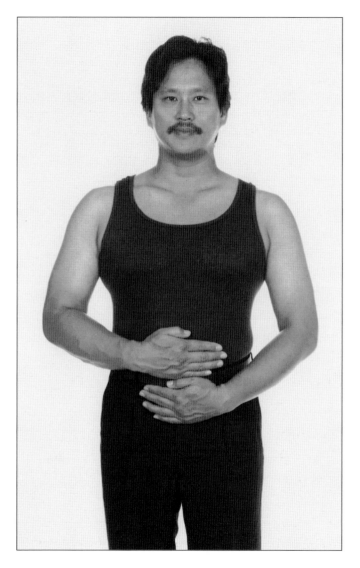

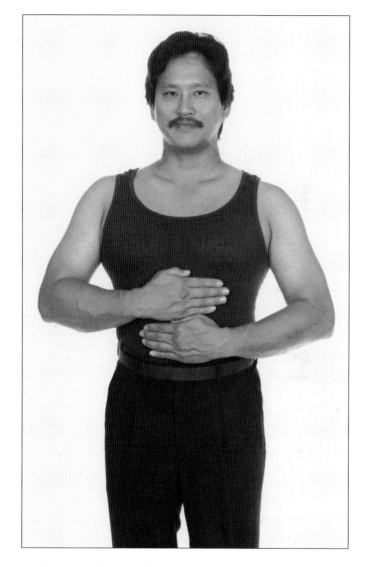

1. Place your hands side by side horizontally on your abdomen one above and one below the navel.

2. Place hands side by side horizontally above the navel between the lower ribs over the solar plexus.

3. Place your hands side by side above the waist over your left lower rib cage.

4. Place your hands side by side below the waist over your left abdomen.

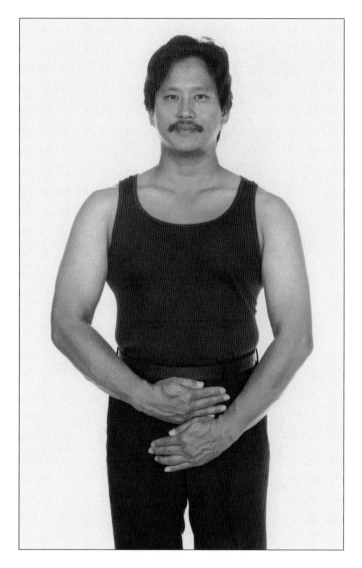

5. Place your hands side by side on and directly above your pubic bone.

6. Place your hands side by side below the waist over your right abdomen.

7. Place your hands side by side above the waist over your right lower rib cage.

8. Place your hands horizontally, side by side between your breasts.

9. Place your hands side by side over your upper chest just below your collarbones.

10. Cup your hands over your eyes, fingers slanting slightly inward and crossing over your forehead.

11. Place your hands on both sides of your head just above your ears, fingers meeting at the top.

12. Place hands side by side horizontally, one above the other covering the lower back of your head.

13. Clasp hands over the throat, one hand above the other, fingers to one side, thumbs to the other.

14. Cross your hands right over left or left over right over your upper chest just below your collarbones.

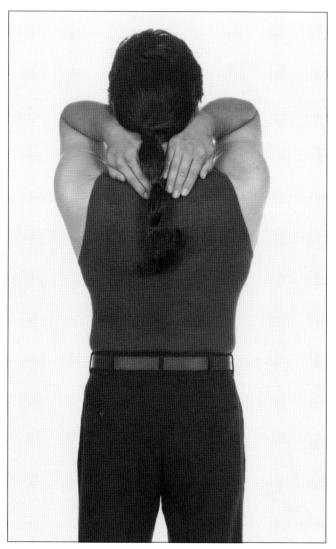

15. Place one hand at the base of the spine and the other hand on the back of the neck.

16. Place hands on the back shoulders near the neck, right hand on right shoulder and left hand on left shoulder, fingers pointing down and inward.

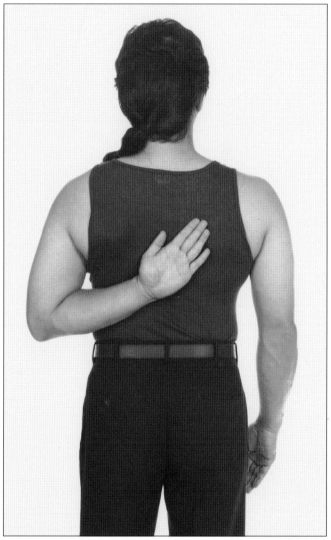

17. Place your left hand behind your back, palm against or away from your right middle-upper back. Repeat with your other hand on opposite side.

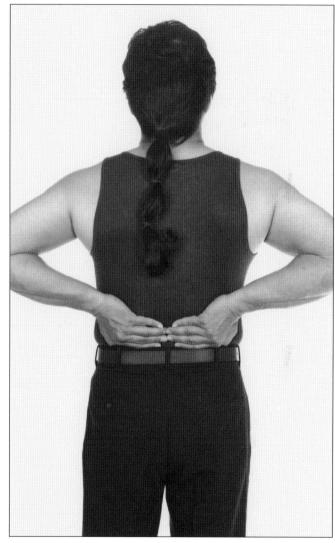

18. Place your hands on each side of the back of your body just above your waist, fingers meeting in the middle at the spine.

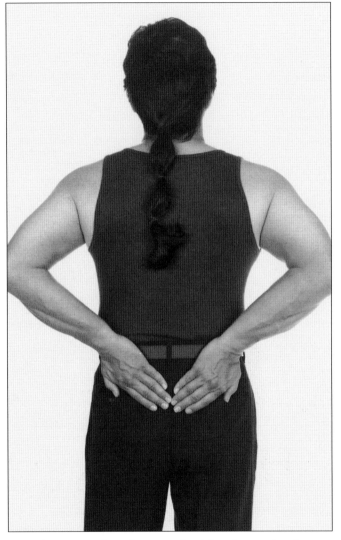

19. Place your hands on each side of your back below the waist, fingers slanted slightly downward, meeting over the spine at the middle-lower back.

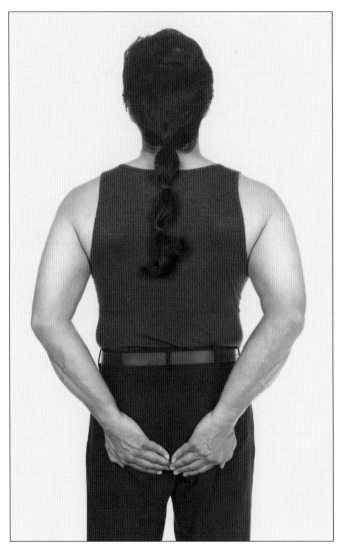

20. Place your hands down lower on either side of your body, fingers slanted slightly downward and meeting at the base of the spine.

REIKI-
Healing
Others

Be a Witness to the Creative Life of Others

Your Full Potential

When treating others, practitioners do not have to believe in what they do;
they need only suspend their beliefs and be willing.
Nor do clients have to believe; they only have to be open.

Doubt, and little else, prevents a free flow of energy.
Doubt and fear are distortions of the mind.
It is not our birthright to have doubt and fear.
It is our challenge, our dis-ease, due to our inheritance.
In our muscles lies the history of humanity's current relationship with its own spirit and with the earth.

To be on this earth, we as spiritual beings have taken form.
Our form is our present orientation in time and space.
This form is our creative limitation and our resistance.
Our resistance limits and allows the number of treatments we are comfortable giving,
the amount of love we are comfortable receiving.

When you treat others and yourself, have no blame;
let the thoughts of the mind pass by
and live true reality ~ love ~ your full potential.

Healing Others

Give Yourself Full Permission to Live at Full Potential

Give yourself full permission to do healing work right now! You do not have to feel you are perfect to begin to heal others. Whether you are well or not, you can do healing work on another. In this game of life, we need all bases covered; it is important to have many kinds of healers at different levels of understanding. People who have a similar understanding and feeling, with whom you resonate, will be drawn to you, and you will be able to learn much from each other. It is wonderful to feel good and to be healthy! Nevertheless, it is not necessary in order to give effective Reiki treatments. When you give Reiki treatments, the client draws universal life energy through you, and you also receive the benefit and cleansing of *reiki*.

Sometimes I gave treatments when congested, and my nose would run with the release of energy; I always felt better after the treatment. When working on a client when I was in this condition, I would say, "If you are not one hundred percent pleased with this treatment, I will give you your money back or do another treatment." They were always satisfied. Be sure to use discretion, however, when treating another. Do not work if you are contagious or exhausted.

Ethics

The most essential ingredients in healing others are your intention to help and the client's desire and permission for you to help. What is a true intention to help? To be successful at healing work, it is best if you

~ give the help that the person desires and that is most appropriate to the moment,

~ remember that your client's life and healing are his or her own responsibility, and

~ go only as far as the client is willing and able to go.

When your client goes further than he or she really wants to go, a resistance or discomfort may be created, and all work moves more slowly, if at all. It may have been too big a step for your client or even an inappropriate one. There could be an incident in his or her life that needs clarification and understanding, or even a person or situation that needs to be forgiven and released before your client is free to move forward. You really have no way of knowing.

If you have an agenda, your client can easily feel that he or she is not fulfilling your expectations. It is good to have ideas and share ideas; however, be sure to allow — even insist — that each person take full responsibility for his or her own healing. When a person is ready to make changes, he or she will, and then you can be there to help in word and deed. In this way you will be successful with your clients every time. It is like the well-known story of the mother chicken who pecks at the egg immediately after the little chick begins pecking and is ready to enter the world.

A client of mine had been going to an excellent chiropractor but was regressing under his care. The chiropractor was so positive about his work that my client began to feel guilty and tense about not getting "well." At this point, she began Reiki treatments with me and started to make some important life decisions. She relaxed, her guilt eased, and the chiropractic work took hold.

Conversely, there are rare cases when a client is not consciously asking for help, yet you feel a strong impulse to suggest a change in lifestyle or habits that may be difficult or painful. That impulse may be part of a new beginning for the person that will mature into realization months, even years, later.

Err on the side of caution.

When something is true, there is no need for hurry.

Let love and acceptance be your faithful companions.

During a Third Level Initiation, I had the impulse to tell a student that as part of her training it would be essential for her to stop smoking. She did stop and began an herbal cleanse, but one month later, preparing for her wedding, she started smoking and abruptly stopped the herbal cleanse. She developed a serious rash and internal heat that took months to resolve. She went everywhere for help except to me. Eventually, she came to me and her anger and rash and heat disappeared during the treatment. Consciously or unconsciously, some force had been used. She had been asked to stop smoking ahead of her natural inclinations.

Factors in Healing

A person's healing depends upon many factors. To attain an optimum level of health, it is helpful to receive bodywork, have proper exercise, a good diet, right thought, and patience. Right thought includes a desire to be well, living by the Reiki Precepts (page 13), a willingness to explore the cause of the illness or stress, and a willingness to make necessary changes. Remember that each individual needs to be addressing these factors in his or her own way.

At an appropriate time, you might want to explore these questions with your client:

Is the problem primarily physical, emotional, mental, or spiritual?

What are the original contributing factors?

Did this illness start at the time of a major life change — divorce, new job, or relocation?

Is the problem chronic or acute?

Are there hidden benefits of this illness?

Does the illness keep the client dependent in some way?

Does the illness keep the client away from a job that he or she doesn't want?

The client's attitude may be only one part of the equation; environmental factors may also play a part. I remember a study in China investigating the prominence of esophageal cancer in one area. The final study showed that people were becoming ill due to the pollution of the drinking water from heavy industry upstream from the city.

So, it is helpful to investigate the client's environment:

> Is your client living in a house that is very damp or moldy?

> Does your client need to be drinking more water or water of better quality?

> Is your client having an allergic response?

It is also essential that the client be eating properly. Ms. Takata stressed a mild diet composed of vegetable juices, vegetables, grains, and perhaps a little fish. This general diet may be found in the book, *Reiki: Hawayo Takata's Story*. We know that Ms. Takata studied not only diet, but also other related fields such as anatomy and hydrotherapy.

At the beginning of my healing practice I studied diet and herbs, but my real interest was the integration of mind, body, and spirit, with particular emphasis on the emotions. I later studied Touch for Health, anatomy, Jin Shin Jyutsu, Bach Flowers, Rebirthing, psychology, and different forms of meditation — Zen, Integral Consciousness Training, Siddha Yoga, Hatha Yoga, and Reiki. These forms of meditation increased the depth of clarity, focus, and love in my work and personal life.

Further education in areas of your own special interests and talents will enhance your practice. In areas in which you have less interest, become a valuable resource person by referring others to professionals in fields such as physical exercise, diet, herbs, massage, homeopathy, chiropractic, counseling, and modern medicine.

Exchanges

You will be most successful in your treatment if your client has already formed the intention to become well. A good situation is for the client to ask you for a treatment and to pay you. This shows a desire on the part of the client to get well and helps keep us as practitioners in business. Barters for goods or services are also a fair exchange, although sometimes bartered goods may need to be thought of as gifts, since you may receive something you would never purchase for yourself. My experience has been that, because you care for the giver, the gift becomes special.

Sometimes a true intention, a deep desire on the part of the client to change, is a sufficient exchange for your help. At other times you may sense a great need on another's part to receive a treatment and there is no request. In these cases, ask if a treatment is desired, and be sure to respect the answer. This respect honors the person's intention. In these ways, you will be successful in your treatments every time.

When I began treating, I would ask friends whom I felt needed help if they would like a treatment. Their response was often, "Oh, you think you can make me better?" or some noncommital response. I then asked friends whom I felt didn't need help, and their response was, "Great!" but they didn't need to continue to come for treatments. From these experiences, I knew how to begin my healing practice. I knew it was important that people who desired treatments had formed the intention to get well and that there was an exchange. After these experiences I began charging money.

Frequency of Treatments

For both chronic and acute problems, it is best to begin by working on your client every day. As you see improvement, begin to treat three times a week, then twice a week. Twice a week is optimum for a continuing problem. Seven days in a row is recommended for people suffering a deep depression or nervous exhaustion. Acute problems are like a sprout or new tree. The roots, like the problems, are near the surface and are easy to dislodge. Chronic problems are like old trees with tangled and gnarled roots that lie deep in the ground; these problems are often deep and entangled within the life of the person and may take longer to clear.

If your client decides to come for treatments only once a week, or as you begin to reduce the frequency of treatments, it is recommended that he or she learn self-help techniques. Reiki training, combined with the tape and this book, are an excellent form of self-help. See the reading list provided at the back of this book for additional forms of self-help. Reiki for the chronically ill was traditionally given on a daily basis, even twice a day. One good solution is for the client's neighbors and friends to learn Reiki and participate in the healing of their loved one.

Ms. Takata, who brought Reiki to this country, suggested that family members work on a chronically ill person every day, twice a day, or even twenty-four hours a day at the start. Treatments might continue for a year. The results were astounding. All manner of serious diseases were successfully treated.

I treated a client who for twelve years had chronically tense shoulders that no amount of therapy or bodywork had substantially reduced. I explained to her that it would be faster and ultimately less costly if we treated daily. We worked every day, and by the end of the third week, her shoulders were softening. We reduced treatments to three times a week for several weeks and finally to twice a week. As her shoulders relaxed, she wandered on the beach and didn't feel like working. Ms. Takata emphasizes in the book Reiki: Hawayo Takata's Story *that it is important to address the cause of an illness. In this case, the woman had a business that she no longer had a genuine interest in owning. Through further counseling, Bach Flower remedies, and energy work, she gained the insight and willpower necessary to develop a new, more appropriate lifestyle.*

The Very Ill

Reiki is ideal for the very ill because the treatments are very gentle and relaxing. Chronically ill people often have sore and tense muscles and tissues, and do not like any pressure. The benefits of a Reiki treatment are great. Clients feel as though they have vigorously exercised, yet there is no risk of strain or exertion. They feel flushed with renewed energy. Their bodies become more balanced, their minds more relaxed, and all body functions are stimulated. Memory improves, the glands work better, and their bodies move more easily. A student who treated his mother every other day reported that she said, "I haven't felt so young since before I got old."

Reducing stress and pain helps the elderly and chronically ill who are meant to transition to do so with greater ease and dignity. *One of my students began giving daily treatments to her dying mother, who was able to stop taking all painkillers until the week before her death.*

Children and Reiki

Children generally have fewer blocks than adults and they release these blocks quickly. Their metabolism and rate of energy are higher, so their treatment times are shorter. When treating children, you may hold the positions for a little less time, add the shortcut for the back (page 112), or do a partial treatment (page 23). Children respond quickly to Reiki treatments. Be sure to have their permission, however, as well as the consent of the parent or guardian.

I treated my twin boys as they grew up and they seldom went to a doctor. All of their specific problems — fevers, colds, earaches, as well as general malaises — were treated successfully in the early stages with energy work, diet, and herbs. Once, at a restaurant, my children ate some food that disagreed with them. Late that night, one after the other woke me up. The first boy I treated relaxed, vomited, and was better immediately. The other boy felt no relief as we worked, yet he was completely better by the next morning. Reiki is an art. There are no guaranteed results. Here we have the same problem with different children and different results.

Most importantly, parents treating children help strengthen deep and important bonds of intimacy and belonging between their children and themselves. Children learn that the loving touch of their guardians also has the potency and wisdom to ease their pain. They feel the deep support and love that are so essential for growth and happiness.

I was visiting with a friend whose teenage daughter had been sick for days. Much to her mother's surprise, her daughter, when asked, said she would love to receive Reiki. The mother, who had no experience with Reiki, joined me in treating her child. At the end, my friend was glowing. "I had the feeling that once again Wendy and I were physically connected, as though my hands were like an umbilical cord and all kinds of power was moving through me to feed and nurture my child again. You lose that feeling as your child grows up! It was so different from a hug." An hour later, my friend went in to see her daughter, who was sitting at her desk working and ready to return to school. Reiki is a wonderful resource to have at first hand.

Reiki benefits everyone. It enables the young, the old, the sick, as well as the healthy and able, to reduce all manner of stress and dis-ease, sudden or accumulated, through the power of their own hands and understanding.

Equipment and the Setting

Blankets

When you do healing work on another person, you will need blankets. As your clients relax, they will often go into a quiet, motionless state, quieter even than sleep. There will be little internal, physical friction in the body and thus less fire and heat, even though their energy is releasing and streaming. They may feel cold. Blankets help your clients feel warm, secure, and comfortable. This comfort will allow them to return to a more original and basic state of mind.

The Setting

It is a luxury to have a quiet room or simply a specific area in a room that is used regularly for meditation and treatments. This space, through continued use, sets the mood and emphasizes the intention for healing, thereby making it easy for the practitioner and client to begin work immediately. *Special conditions are not necessary, however. I can remember working on people while tile-setters were cutting ceramic tiles with a buzz saw in the next room. I was amazed that once the treatment began concentration was no problem at all. It is as if the healing work opens us to an inner space where even what we often consider noise becomes music.*

A Massage Table

It is an advantage to have a massage table, so that when the client lies face down, the head can be placed straight down in the face cradle instead of to the side. Purchase a table that stands at a comfortable working height. The table, like the room, helps create a mood and sets the intention for healing. Please remember, however, that much good work has been done on a couch, bed, or chair. Simply make yourself and your client as comfortable as possible. Even if you do not have special equipment you can give wonderful and effective treatments.

Guidelines

Become as Comfortable as You Can

Doing Reiki treatments is a definite physical accomplishment. For long periods of time you will have your hands extended in front of you. For your comfort, you might need to rest your hands on the client, the table, pillows, or even parts of yourself such as your thighs or knees. You may sit, stand, or even kneel at the side of your client. When sitting, the height of the chair or stool in relation to the height of the table or bed will make a big difference to your comfort in giving Reiki treatments. Take the time to discover which positions and equipment work best for you.

Begin Your Treatment

Begin your treatment with a prayer or positive thought to still the mind, or simply empty yourself, become quiet, and begin to treat. Remain quiet. The key to healing with Reiki is to just be. Let all body sensations and thoughts pass through you. Sometimes the treatment may trigger discomfort or anxiety within you. Let these sensations pass. If you experience comfort, bliss, or joy, let these sensations pass as well. Relax and allow all thought, sensation, and sound to flow through your body/mind as you enter into this deep meditation with another person. Becoming centered in this way, a witness to your own thoughts and possibly the client's thoughts, you enter into a state of healing for yourself and others, and you will not carry away any problems that may surface during the treatment.

If, during treating, you find you have thoughts and sensations that are not your usual ones, they may relate to your client's experience of life. You may choose to let these thoughts go or you may feel the information would be valuable to your client. Ask your client if he or she would like to know what you are feeling or receiving about them and the treatment. Tell your client that this input may be colored by your own mind and to please take what you say "with a grain of salt." Let your client decide if and in what way the information is significant.

In Reiki, we teach this paradox: "Thinking by keeping in the deep part of the mind." This is really not thinking at all, just a deep inner knowing. In Christian terms it is the "peace that surpasseth all understanding." Allow your "conversation" to come from that deep, easy space.

Ask for Feedback

If you have questions while treating another, ask for feedback. It is best to get feedback as to hand pressure and placement and answers to other questions you might have at the beginning of the treatment when your client is the most awake and available. You can ask your client, "Which position feels best? Do you like my hands placed right over left or left over right, or side by side, or one hand in front of the other?" Tell clients to feel free to tell you at any time during the treatment if they want more or less pressure, or your hands in a slightly different position. Tell them that you may immediately move your hands, or if an area is still releasing tension, you will move your hands after you have finished working on that position.

At the end of the treatment, ask your clients to choose an area on their body that they feel needs a little more attention and finish by working on that area. Sit on their left side — the feminine, receptive side. When they turn over onto their stomach, move to the other side. You are now again on their left side. If you have any doubts as to which side feels best for them, ask. In the healing state you will naturally and intuitively begin to access your knowing mind. In this simple mode of healing it is best to do what your intuition tells you, combined with information from your clients.

Schedule Plenty of Time

A Reiki treatment generally takes about an hour. It is important to allow an extra half hour for introductory and completion time. Allow time at the beginning to find out about the client's progress, and time at the end to talk about the treatment and any self-care to be done before the next treatment. It is my preference to schedule every two hours so that I have a half hour of quiet time between treatments. This also ensures extra time for my clients if need be.

Here are some thoughts from a student that highlight the healing principles outlined in this chapter:

"David, who worked with me in the office and was just beginning to learn some Reiki, was helping me give Marsha a treatment. During this treatment I discovered that the principles of sitting comfortably, letting your mind become empty, and staying with the energy are of utmost importance. David was sitting in a slump, and his back had grown tired and painful a few minutes into treating. Marsha suggested that he sit more comfortably. It was suggested that he adjust his head and neck by allowing them to move forward and upward and allow his back to lengthen and widen while he found a comfortable sitting position. His hands immediately heated up and his back pain went away. Later in the treatment, I noticed pulsating surges from his hands. Upon inquiry, it turned out that he was letting his mind wander and felt distracted by his thoughts. When he quieted his mind, let his thoughts come and go, and focused on the energy or the feeling of treating, the quality of the treatment improved ninety percent. The feeling from his hands became steady, soft, and directed, which made the treatment powerful and enjoyable."

Information for Your Client

Each new client may require a slightly different introduction to Reiki. Some people want to know about Reiki and the treatments they will be receiving before they start, others like to know about you, and some people just like to begin and go for the experience. At the beginning, it is usually best to briefly introduce the art, yourself, and ask for their history — any physical, mental, or emotional problems, current or past, and the types of medical or alternative treatments they may have had. It is also wise to explore their expectations. The information you gather helps you understand how Reiki treatments best serve them. Be sure to tell them that you are doing an overall treatment for general relaxation and stress reduction. You are not attempting to cure a specific problem. Do not attempt to diagnose a condition or prescribe unless you have the appropriate license.

The Treatment

Inform your clients that treatments will take about an hour, that they begin on the front of the body and end on the back, and that they will be fully clothed without shoes, belts, or jewelry. Tell them that in a Reiki treatment there is usually little pressure. In fact, treatments are so gentle they may feel as though they are entering a waking dream state. In this relaxed state, all movements such as turning over or getting up are best done slowly. This method, because it is so very gentle, is excellent for the elderly, children, and the very sick. It is also good for subtle alignment, as well as chronic dis-ease.

Let your clients know that they are free to talk, wiggle, giggle, move, or take a bathroom or water break. Tell them that if you have to leave for a moment it will not interrupt the flow of the treatment. In fact, they will have a chance to rest and integrate what has been done; the treatment will then continue on a deeper level. If your clients eat before their treatment, ask them please to eat only lightly so that their energy flows freely.

Although Reiki treatments are gentle and ultimately further only the change that the client truly desires, there may be an initial cleansing of old patterns in order to make way for the new. A person may feel worse for a short while as physical toxins are released from storage places in the cells and old thoughts and pictures surface for review and release. If this happens, treating your client for two or three days in a row is highly recommended. Suggest that your client rest and drink plenty of water to flush the system. Sometimes having your client talk about feelings with a practitioner or friend will help them integrate this new release of energy. After this cleansing, the client often feels clearer and more energetic and experiences a deeper sense of well-being.

Reiki is an art: there is no one answer for all people and all situations. I remember working on a friend. After the treatment, he said that he did not like Reiki very much. I spontaneously said, "I think maybe you do not like yourself very much at this moment." I meant that he did not like the thoughts and feelings he was having. He came back for two or three more treatments, those uncomfortable tensions dissipated, and he decided that he liked Reiki very much.

Attitude

Ask your clients to let their minds drift and to simply notice their thoughts. In this waking dream state, thoughts, pictures, and sensations will pass through their consciousness. Tell them not to build with these pictures and thoughts. An example of building your thoughts would be "I have so much to do today," then thinking "If I drop the car off, that will give me more time for . . . Oh, I forgot. Susan is coming over today," etc. Instead, tell them to let each thought pass, and feel the accompanying body sensations (maybe a jittery feeling or warm feeling). Then let those sensations pass as well. This is the practice of letting the mind and body settle and allows your clients to experience the treatment and themselves directly. In addition, suggest that during the treatment they not concentrate on their breathing or any environmental sounds.

This open state of mind will help a client to let go at a deeper level. Different sensations may occur upon entering into this state of deep relaxation. For example, muscles might jump spontaneously or a slight electrical shock may be felt as energy surges to different areas. Blocked areas previously unrecognized might reveal themselves as the body lets go and relaxes. Reiki treatments work nonspecifically on the body as a whole; even so, the release of a particularly tense point, like the opening of a floodgate, may allow the whole body to let go. As the body opens to this freer flow of energy, your client has the opportunity to experience delightful feelings of love, ease, warmth, even deep coolness. As relaxation deepens, various pleasurable feelings may move up the spine or across the body. Gradually, your client will fully enjoy and even look forward to being in the moment in this relaxed way.

Talking

Tell your clients that they are free to talk. Be sure that their speech comes from deep within them, that they are not talking to avoid the feeling and possible release of some deep tension or pain. If it sounds as though they are talking anxiously, ask them to please relax and talk from their bones, cells, or from deep inside themselves. Talking may be a necessary and important part of their release.

I remember working with one client, holding a hand position on her shoulder for a very long time; that point did not fully open until she began to talk about her problems at work.

Tell your clients that you might be talking to them as well. You might ask for feedback on the hand positions, or you might have something important to communicate that will help them relax more or discover something further about themselves. Apart from these kinds of exchanges, a Reiki treatment is usually conducted in silence.

Sound

You may want to ask if your client would like music during the treatment. Music creates a powerful healing force. The type of music you select sets up a field of energy that greatly influences you and your client's experience. Be sure you wish to direct the experience that way and be sensitive to your client's reactions as well. *Although some people relax best with music, I usually work without it. When I feel someone would really do best with music, I select music carefully with the sole purpose of helping that particular client to let go.*

Vibration is the creative dance of the universe. Sound is vibration at frequencies that we can hear and is the basis of most ancient healing systems. Through the science of sound we can alter ourselves, and thus create the universe that we truly desire. Sacred sounds, called mantras in the East and prayers in the West, protect and heal the mind by aligning it to a higher source. The sacred sounds of Reiki have the potent function of harmonizing the physical, mental, emotional, and spiritual bodies so that universal life energy flows easily through us.

Confidentiality

Tell your clients that whatever transpires during the treatment is confidential. It is important that clients feel secure enough to say whatever is on their minds, for this helps them to relax into the treatment completely. Their comfort may depend on your assurances that anything discussed with you, even if it is minor, will not be discussed with others.

Reiki and Modern Medical Care

Be sure to tell your client that this work is not considered a substitute for medical care. Diagnosis and prescription are not part of a Reiki treatment. You might also suggest that your client find a doctor who has an interest in natural healing to enhance cooperation between these two approaches. The work you are doing is an overall body treatment designed to encourage optimum health and to release physical, emotional, and mental blocks.

The people we treat are healers calling upon us to help them on their journey. This journey is their creation. We are as much learning and being healed by them as they are by us. It is important to give the power back to the client. I remember a client who felt so good during a particular treatment that he said to me, "You are so very powerful. I can really feel your power." I said, "What you feel is you at a deeper level. I am simply helping you clear the energy blocks that cause you to live at less than your full power."

It is very important that clients understand that what they feel is both what they are manifesting and also what they are bringing into manifestation.

Many people like to say this healing power is only coming through us. I would like to say we are this healing power, each and every one of us, when we live light, love, and power.

> *"I clothe myself with a robe of light*
> *composed of love, power, and wisdom*
> *enveloping and interpenetrating me*
> *not only for my own protection*
> *but so that all who see it and come in contact with it*
> *will be drawn to the Light*
> *and healed."*

Robe of Light Prayer *adapted from*
It Is ALL Right *by Isabel M. Hickey.*

Reminders

We are all healers.

> *We not only allow love to come through us ~ we are love.*

We do not heal another.

> *The primary source of healing is always within each of us.*

When treating, have as little judgment as possible. Do no-thing.

> *Be every-thing. Surrender to the fullness of the moment.*

Healing is often an up-and-down process.

> *Two steps forward, one step back gives our consciousness time to clearly observe our life.*

> *This produces a strong interlocking stitch that will never tear apart again.*

Experience an instantaneous healing.

> *Create a life with no seams, no ups and downs.*

> *Remain in the eternal moment, where all is possible.*

Treating ourselves and others is a reminder of our natural state.

> *It is important to bring this healing energy of love, "reiki," into our daily lives.*

The Basics

In Reiki healing, we are not directing specific energy into the body; rather, we are letting go and allowing. We live an active state of beingness. When treating others there is nothing to do. It is a paradox: you do nothing and yet everything is done effortlessly. Please do not daydream or think. Instead let your knowing mind "think" you; let your thoughts and feelings come and go and you will enter into a healing state of awareness. It is natural to wonder, "Is this working?" yet the only thing you can do that is "not working" is to think or doubt while treating another.

Your clients will also help you to achieve this healing state by being there with you. Your clients, by relaxing and letting their thoughts come and go, will naturally draw healing, continuous universal life energy through you to where they have the greatest need. Reiki treatments, with their potent hand positions, open up channels in the body so that universal life energy flows abundantly. Just as water naturally flows downhill, universal energy naturally flows to areas where there is a deficiency or need. The healer's hands often get warm and then begin to cool as the client opens to the increased flow of energy. Remember we have been called human be-ings: this is a great truth.

A treatment position is generally held for five minutes. The head positions — eyes, crown, and back of head — are often held for a longer time and set the tone for the whole treatment. The Head Flow Pattern reduces mental tensions by relaxing the eyes, balances the right and left sides of the body, and harmonizes the chakra and endocrine systems.

When you first learn to treat, time yourself or watch a clock. Later on, use your intuition. Most importantly, make yourself comfortable, rest your hands gently on the person, and do not move your hands while they are warming up. From the alternatives on the following pages, pick the hand position that feels most comfortable to you.

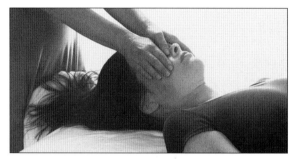

1. *The Brow Chakra   p. 98*

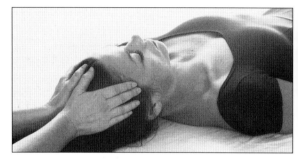

2. *The Crown Chakra   p. 99*

5. *The Transpersonal Heart   p. 102*

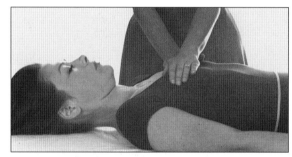

6. *The Heart Chakra   p. 103*

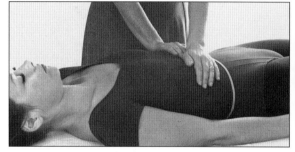

7. *The Solar Plexus Chakra   p. 104*

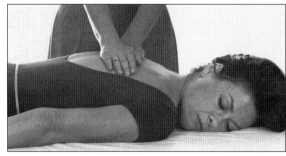

11. *The Heart Chakra   p. 108*

12. *The Solar Plexus Chakra   p. 109*

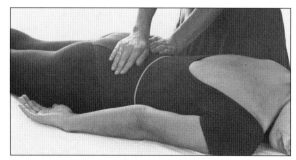

13. *The Sacral Chakra   p. 110*

3. The Base Brain p. 100

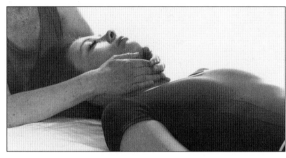

4. The Throat Chakra p. 101

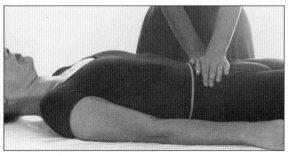

8. The Sacral Chakra p. 105

9. The Base Chakra p. 106

10. The Transpersonal Heart p. 107

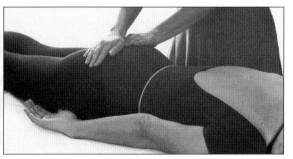

14. The Base Chakra p. 111

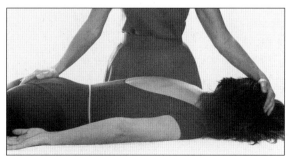

15. The Coccyx to Head or Back of Neck p. 112

16. The Feet p. 113

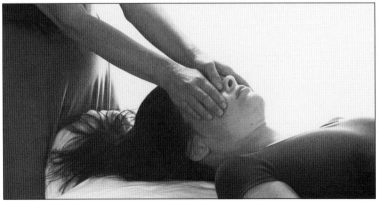

First Position:

The Brow Chakra

Place your hands gently over the client's closed eyes. Your palms are resting on the forehead and your fingers are cupped over the eyes with the tips of your fingers touching the cheekbones. Fingers are placed straight up and down. You may also slant your fingers slightly outward over the eyes, crossing your thumbs right over left or left over right. Your thumbs are doubled over the space between the eyebrows — the third eye. The client's eyes will be in darkness. Be careful not to push on the nostrils so he/she can breathe freely.

Second Position:

The Crown Chakra

Place the base of your palms over the top center of the head, the crown chakra. Your fingers reach downward toward the ears, and in some cases over them. Fingers may be apart or closed, depending on your preference.

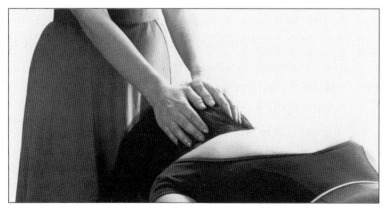

Third Position:

The Base Brain

Roll the head very gently to the left and place your right hand under the right back head, fingertips reaching downward, touching where the head and neck meet. Then roll the head gently over onto the right hand and place your left hand on the left back of the head. Again, fingertips will be touching where the head and neck meet. Roll the head gently back to center over both hands. Hands are now placed side by side vertically and fingers are together or slightly apart reaching downward.

When finishing this position, gently slide your hands away from the head or gently roll the head off your hands. The head is surprisingly heavy. Make all of your movements gentle so you do not rouse the client from this relaxed state.

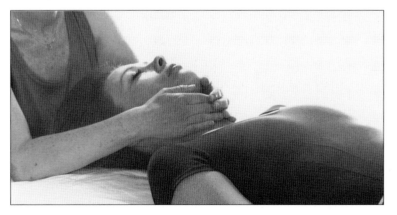

Fourth Position:

The Throat Chakra

Remain at the head and gently place your hands over the client's throat by crossing your fingers left over right or right over left, hands covering the whole throat. For people who do not like their necks to be touched, rest the sides of your little fingers on the collarbones and the sides of your thumbs on the jawbones, fingers meeting or crossing in the middle of the throat. You will then be covering the whole throat without touching it directly.

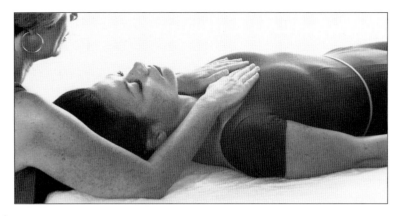

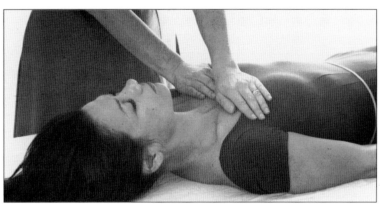

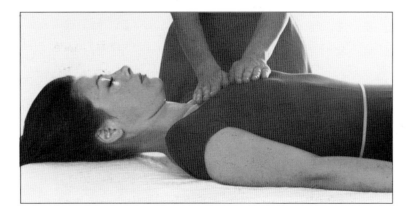

Fifth Position:

The Transpersonal Heart

Remain at the client's head and place your hands on the upper chest. Your palms will be resting just below the collarbones, your fingers together or slightly apart, reaching downward and slanting slightly inward. Alternatively, you may move to the person's left side and place one hand in front of the other spanning the body, fingers touching the base of the palm of the hand in front, directly under the collarbones. Another position is to place your hands side by side horizontally, or cross your hands (not shown) left over right or right over left in the middle of the upper chest just below the collarbones.

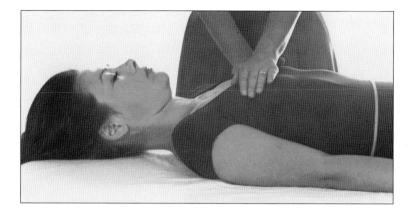

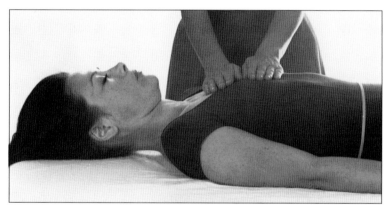

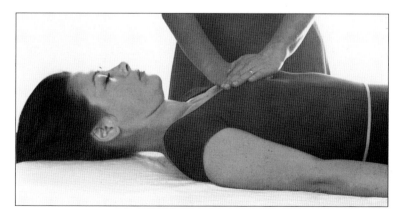

Sixth Position:

The Heart Chakra

Standing or sitting at the client's left side, place your hands over the tops of the breasts, fingers touching the base of the palm of the hand in front. Or you may place your hands side by side horizontally, or cross your hands right over left or left over right in the center of the chest between the breasts. Pick the position that you feel is most comfortable for you and your client.

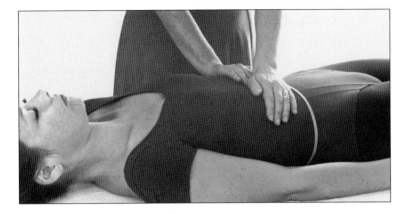

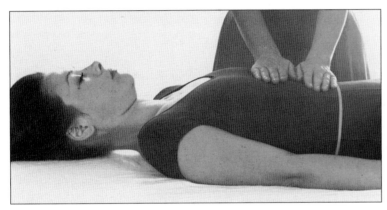

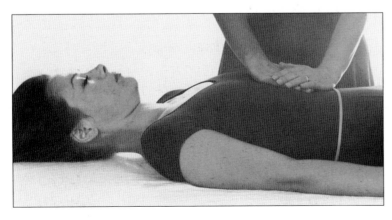

Seventh Position:

The Solar Plexus Chakra

Place your hands above the navel. The lower edges of your hands are placed an inch or so above the navel, one hand in front of the other, fingers touching the base of the palm of the hand in front. As an alternative, place your hands side by side horizontally, or cross your hands right over left or left over right in the middle of the lower rib cage.

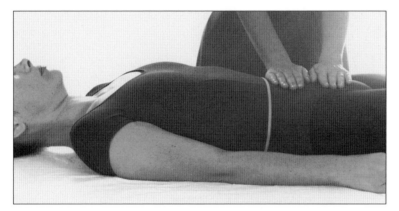

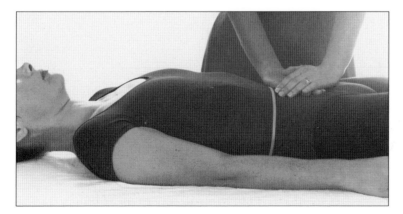

Eighth Position:

The Sacral Chakra

Place your hands an inch or so below the navel, one hand in front of the other, fingers touching the base of the palm of the hand in front. As an alternative, place your hands side by side horizontally, or cross your hands left over right or right over left over the lower abdomen.

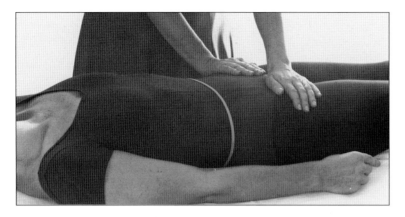

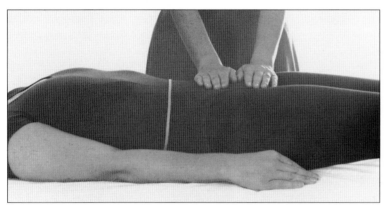

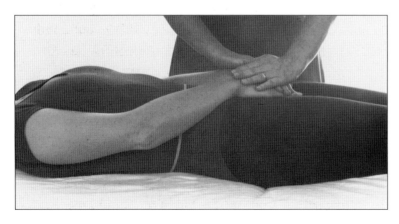

Ninth Position:

The Base Chakra

Place your hands horizontally along the sides of the client's pubic bone, where the legs meet the torso. Alternatively, place your hands side by side over the abdomen and then, to ensure privacy, slide your hands down to the pubic bone. Another alternative is to place the client's hands or ask the client to place his/her hands over the pubic bone. Then place your hands on top of his/her hands.

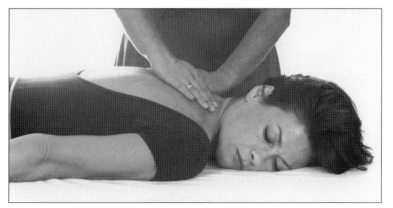

Tenth Position:

The Transpersonal Heart

Have the client turn over onto his/her stomach. Move to the left side of the client. Place your hands on the shoulders, one hand in front of the other, fingers touching the base of the palm of the hand in front. As an alternative, place your hands on either side of the neck, the hand closest to you pointing downward with palm resting on the top of the shoulder, and the hand furthest away pointing upward with palm on the client's back and fingertips resting on the top of the shoulders.

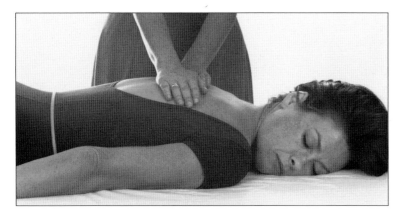

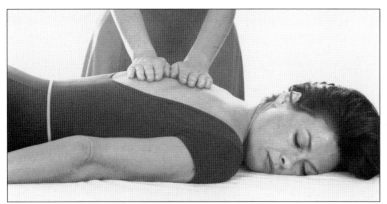

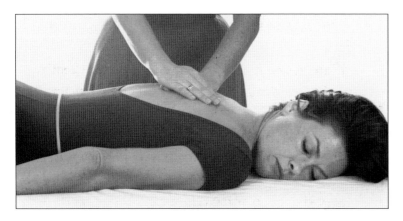

Eleventh Position:

The Heart Chakra

Place your hands on the middle of the upper
back, one hand in front of the other, fingers touching
the base of the palm of the hand in front.
As an alternative, gently place your hands side by
side horizontally across the body, or cross your
hands right over left or left over right in the middle
of the upper back over the spine.

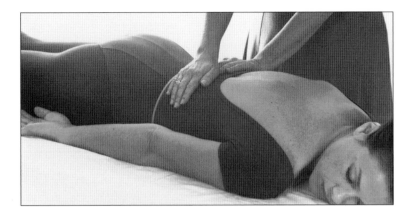

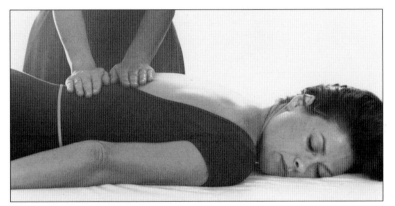

Twelfth Position:

The Solar Plexus Chakra

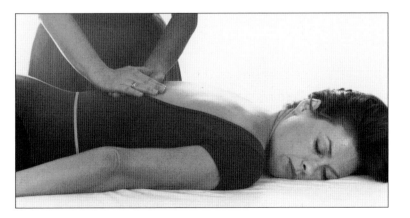

Place your hands an inch or so above the client's waist, one hand in front of the other, fingers touching the base of the palm of the hand in front. Or you may place your hands side by side horizontally, or gently cross your hands right over left or left over right in the middle of the back over the spine. Your hands are opposite the solar plexus.

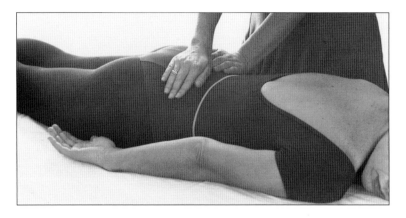

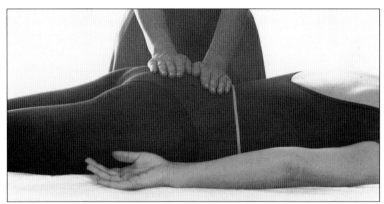

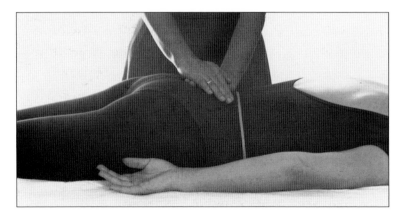

Thirteenth Position:

The Sacral Chakra

Place your hands an inch or so below the waist, one hand in front of the other, fingers touching the base of the palm of the hand in front. Or you may place your hands side by side horizontally, or cross your hands right over left or left over right in the middle of the lower back below the waist.

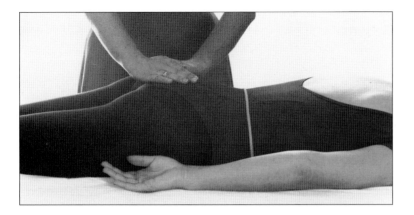

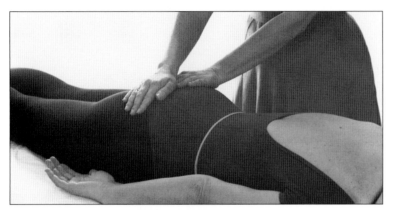

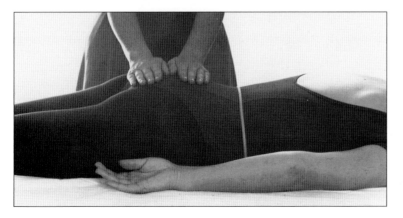

Fourteenth Position:

The Base Chakra

Gently cross your hands right over left or left over right on the coccyx — the tiny bones at the end of the spine. As an alternative, place your hands one hand in front of the other, fingers meeting the base of the palm of the hand in front, covering the coccyx and lower buttocks. You may also place your hands side by side horizontally over the central part of the lower back, covering the coccyx and sacrum.

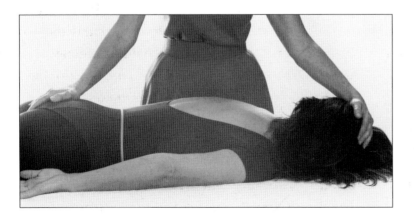

Optional Position:

The Coccyx to Head or Back of Neck

To complete the back treatment, place your right hand on the coccyx and your left hand on the top of the head or over the back of the neck. Hold for a few minutes. This integrates the flow of energy throughout the back and spinal column.

Now ask if there is a spot on the body, front or back, that needs just a little more attention. Hold your hands there for as long as you like.

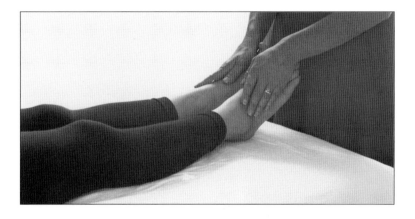

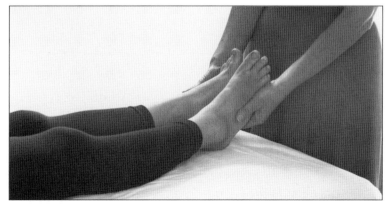

Fifteenth Position:

The Feet

At the end of the treatment the client will be on his/her front or back. Place your hands on the tops or bottoms of the feet. Hold for a few minutes.

On the back of the body, place your hands along the sides of the neck and slowly draw your hands down the sides of the back approximately one inch away from the spine. On the front of the body, draw your hands over the body approximately one inch away from the spine, with your hands not touching the body to ensure privacy. Continue this movement down the legs and end by resting your hands on the bottoms or tops of the feet. This continuous pass, done three times, integrates the flow of energy throughout the whole body and helps the client feel more grounded. If the client feels dizzy upon standing, ask the client to breathe slowly and to imagine the breath going down into the feet.

Photo-Instructions for the Stomach Flow Treatment

The Stomach Flow Pattern treats shock and promotes good digestion and elimination. The hand positions begin in the center of the abdomen, travel clockwise around the abdomen and up to the heart area between the breasts. The hands then move to the head positions, beginning with the eyes, and travel back down to the heart. Complete the treatment by doing the back positions. For more complete descriptions of the head and back positions, turn to Photo-Instructions for the Head Flow on pages 30-59. The model on this page is the person giving the Stomach Flow Treatment. His posture portrays a healing state of mind.

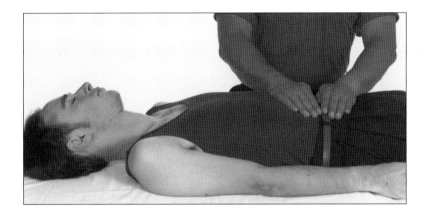

1. Place your hands side by side on the client's abdomen, one above and one below the navel.

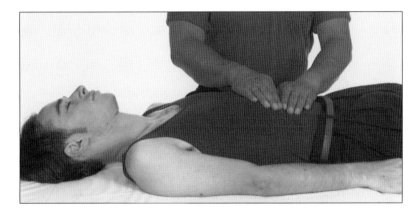

2. Place your hands side by side above the navel between the lower ribs.

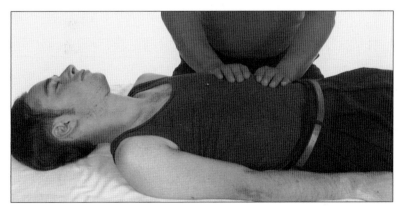

3. Place your hands side by side over the left lower rib cage.

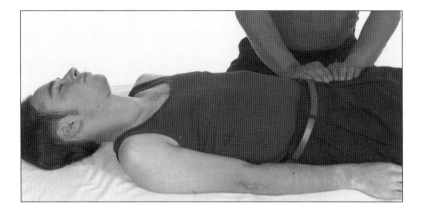

4. Place your hands side by side below the waist over the left abdomen.

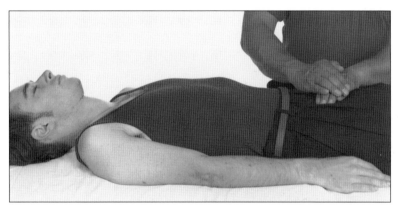

5. Place your hands side by side or cross your hands right over left or left over right in the center of the abdomen above the pubic bone.

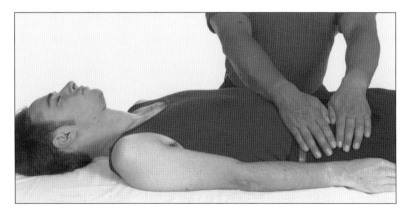

6. Place your hands side by side below the waist over the right abdomen.

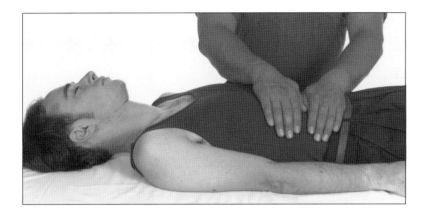

7. Place your hands side by side below the breast over the right lower rib cage.

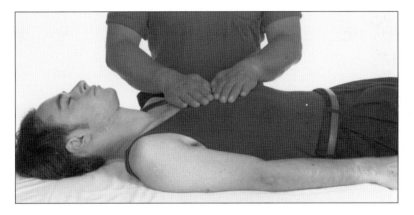

8. Place your hands side by side or cross your hands left over right or right over left between the breasts.

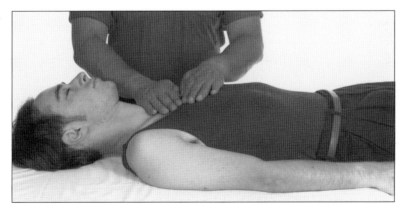

9. Place your hands side by side or cross your hands right over left or left over right in the center of the chest just below the collarbones.

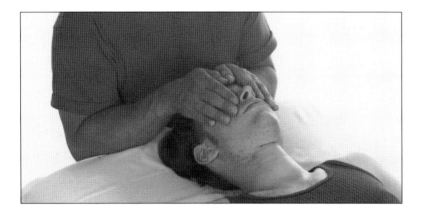

10. Move up to the top of the client's head and place your hands gently over the closed eyes. Your palms will be resting on the forehead, your fingers cupped over the eyes. Fingers are placed straight up and down or slanting slightly outward, thumbs doubled over the space between the eyebrows and the forehead.

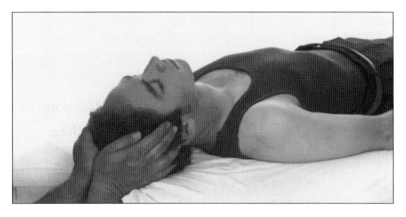

11. Place the base of your palms over the top center of the head, the crown chakra. Your fingers will be reaching downward toward the ears and even at times over the ears.

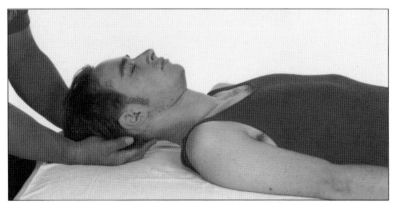

12. Roll the head gently to the left and place your right hand under the right back of the head, fingertips touching where the head and neck meet. Roll the head gently over onto your right hand and place your left hand on the left back of the head. Roll the head carefully back to center over both hands. To finish, slowly slide your hands away.

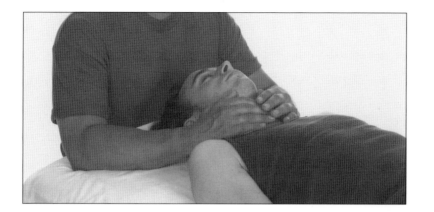

13. Remain seated at the client's head and gently place your hands over the throat by crossing your hands left over right or right over left, hands covering the whole throat.

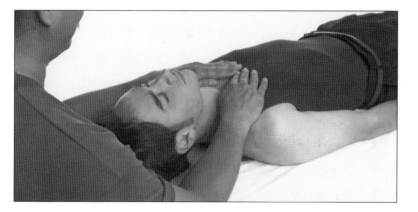

14. Remain seated at the head and place your hands on the upper chest. Your palms will be resting just below the collarbones, fingers together or slightly apart, reaching downward and slanting slightly inward.

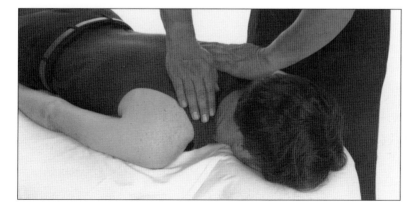

15. Move on the left side of the client. Place your hands on either side of the neck with the hand closest to you pointing downward, palm resting on top of the shoulder, and the hand farther away pointing upward, palm on the client's back and fingertips resting on top of the shoulders.

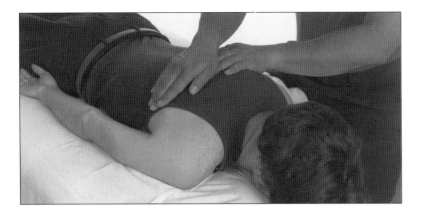

16. Place your hands on the middle of the upper back, one hand in front of the other, fingers touching the base of the palm of the hand in front.

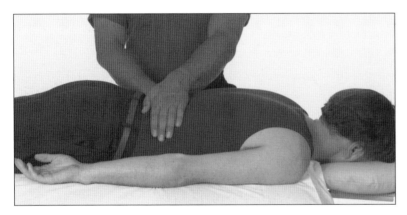

17. Place your hands an inch or so above the client's waist, one hand in front of the other, fingers touching the base of the palm of the hand in front.

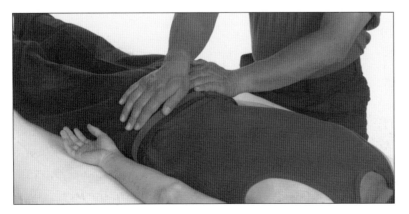

18. Place your hands an inch or so below the waist, one hand in front of the other, fingers touching the base of the palm of the hand in front.

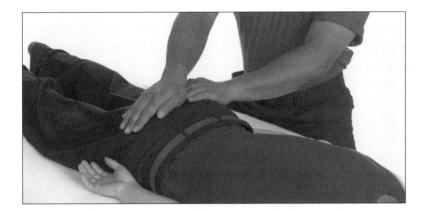

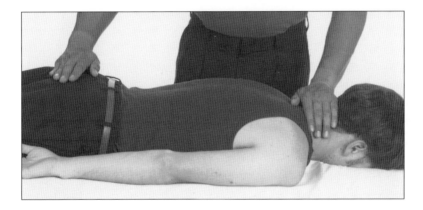

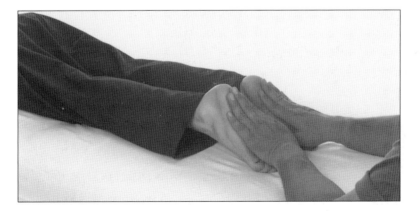

19. Gently place your hands, one hand in front of the other, fingers touching the base of the palm of the hand in front, covering the buttocks and the coccyx — the tiny bones at the end of the spine.

20. To finish the treatment, gently place your right hand on the coccyx and your left hand on the back of the neck or top of the head.

21. Then, place your hands along each side of the client's neck and slowly draw your hands down each side of the body approximately one inch away from the spine. Continue this movement down the legs and end by resting your hands on the bottom of the feet. Ask your client to breathe slowly and to imagine the breath going down into the feet.

122

Testimonials

I *include experiences of some of my students so that you, as practitioners and students of healing, can better understand the many applications of Reiki and hands-on healing. When reading the testimonials, please do not expect that you will necessarily have identical experiences. Each one of us is unique and different, and each situation also has its own special character. Take these stories as inspirations and possibilities.*

Kay Littau

Office Manager

My first surprise in the class was finding out you could use it on yourself. I thought it was just for other people. With two major illnesses in my family in less than a year, I can't describe the comfort that doing Reiki for them gives me. Mom says she feels like floating Jell-O when we're through. I started working on her in the recovery room after her surgery. I used it with her daily for three weeks. When the nurses read her vital signs after a treatment, whatever had been previously high or low (temperature or blood pressure) was then reading normal. It calmed her when she was upset and allowed her to think things out, rather than just reacting. It was a great blessing for her.

I have found the training to be of great use to me, too. The main thing I have learned is that I must use my heart more in dealing with myself and others.

Richard Ruback

Carpenter Supervisor

For me, Reiki was a way for our whole family to communicate in a loving and healing way. My mother was suffering from a pinched nerve and so she was the focus of the treatment, but my father and I who were the "healers" benefited as well. My experience was a consistent and strong flow of love throughout my inner being. The whole family became more and more mellow and gentle.

Phyllis Dryer

Since taking Reiki Level One, some remarkable changes have taken place in my health. I had suffered from migraine headaches for thirty-five years. I was never sure what would bring one on, but they were worse in hot, humid weather. Eight years ago I began taking Inderol for them, which helped tremendously. I'm not comfortable taking drugs, however, and tried from time to time to "wean" myself from them, but the headaches always returned.

Since learning Reiki and practicing it daily, I am off Inderol completely. Occasionally I have a headache, but not the debilitating ones that totally incapacitated me as before.

Reiki has also freed me from the bothersome habit of needing laxatives, another "lifelong" condition. With just these two immediate results from the daily practice of this simple technique, I feel the possibilities of achieving and maintaining radiant health are very real and within the grasp of anyone willing to learn the Reiki method.

Elin Evans
Schoolteacher

My son Chadd fell from the roof of a two-story building and sustained a head injury. He was unconscious for the first two weeks in intensive care and developed pneumonia within the first twenty-four hours. He was heavily sedated to keep the pressure on his brain from elevating while the rest of his body was fighting the pneumonia.

About this time, Marsha Burack introduced me to Reiki hands-on healing. She invited my husband and me to her home and initiated us into Reiki and Reiki hands-on healing techniques. The mental and emotional release (and relief!) I felt at being able to help my son through the positive action of touch was very beneficial to me and to Chadd. I believe that his healing process was immediately enhanced physically, mentally, and emotionally through these treatments. His temperature dropped, and he seemed less agitated and more at peace with himself when my husband and/or I were working on him. After two weeks in intensive care, and within twenty-four hours after beginning treatments, he came out of his coma and was taken off the respirator. He is currently involved in the process of rehabilitation.

I'm very thankful and grateful to Marsha for her time, her knowledge, and certainly for the moral support she has given to our family during this time.

Cheryl Gould
Herbalist/Model/Advertising Specialist

I am pleased with my recent experience with Reiki. I felt a definite shift in consciousness after the initiation and have been enjoying continuing success with each new healing experience. My daughters and I have found the audio tape to be very powerful and we use it regularly.

I first became interested in Reiki several years ago after receiving an amazing healing that dispelled severely swollen glands and strep throat in less than an hour. At the time, I found it hard to believe how this could be possible; however, the reality was that it had happened to me. I knew that it was real.

My first hands-on experience was with my daughter Cathy. She had been suffering with a respiratory infection for several days and was having bouts of severe coughing that kept her awake at night. I gave her a full Reiki treatment, and within an hour she was feeling much better and the cough was greatly relieved.

My next experience was with my other daughter Chris. The circumstances were very similar but more interesting, considering that for years she has suffered with a chronic cough that sometimes lasts for months. We began Reiki and an herbal remedy, and within twenty-four hours she was completely well. I am very happy with this new complement to my healing experience.

Rebecca Brown
Writer/Artist

Two days after I had received First Level from Marsha, my mother was stung hard by wasps on both hands. She has chronic lung disease and is so allergic to wasp venom that she reacts with much pain, severe swelling that can last for weeks, and respiratory and heart complications. It's a serious situation for her, and this was our first experience with Reiki in an emergency. I treated her throughout that day, both full body and spot treatments to her hands. She had immediate pain relief, and there was only minimal swelling, which went down completely by the second day. Her heart and breathing were never affected at all.

I thought later, sometimes you can believe in a thing, and sometimes you can even know it deep in your bones, all without proof, and yet when the proof comes it overwhelms you anyway and feels like a miracle. Reiki is that, I think: a very practical miracle.

Faith Damask

Calligrapher/Reiki Teacher

My very first experience practicing Reiki was on two of my friends, Alison and Matt. Their favorite cat was killed in front of their house when it darted into traffic.

Alison described her pain to me, saying, "I actually feel a pain in my chest, as if my heart were breaking." Matt described his nightly nightmare of his neighbor coming to his door after the accident and saying, "Is this your cat?"

A few days after the treatments, Alison called me and said, "Matt and I slept straight through the night. We didn't move! And although I still miss my cat, my heart has been mended. That terrible chest pain is gone."

Becky Wardrip

Health Food Store Manager

When I first started this class, I had an idea of what I thought Reiki would be about. I thought it would be a learning experience for everyone. But you learn more about yourself in three weeks than you ever imagined possible. Sometimes it is hard to be that close to yourself. Memories from the past come to you, and you realize how much other people's actions and words affect you. Then you realize how you affect other people just with simple words. Even if you don't feel like you are accomplishing something during your self-treatments, you will begin to set things in motion, and over a period of time your views on life will take on new meanings, and you will grow to new awareness.

I didn't always like treating myself. It is very easy to focus on other people. I felt a lot of anger, bliss, sorrow, insecurity, and great courage. It is important to realize that a person is many emotions and realities all wrapped into one, not necessarily at the same time.

Kathy Yttsu

Secretary

Reiki has helped me to open up the flow of energy throughout my body. It has helped me attain a centeredness that I have never felt before on an ongoing basis. And the simplicity of the technique is amazing!

Brandy

Elementary Teacher

I teach elementary school; I have thirty-one children in my class. After waking up at 5:30 a.m. and dealing with all these children (little mirrors), most days I come home exhausted mentally and physically, my mind going around in circles with concerns, problems, and worries.

When I come home, I lie down on the floor and put my hands on my head and do Reiki for ten to thirty minutes. Most of the time I fall asleep while treating myself.

When I am through, I wake (or get) up refreshed, clear, and peaceful. I do Reiki on myself every day. After years of self-hypnosis, meditation, and T'ai Chi, I've found this form to be the most helpful and healing.

George Cossolias

Accountant/Healer

Reiki is the manifestation of simple touch. Touch is not only the physical process of making a connection with others, but the awareness of the interconnectedness that we truly have with each other. Reiki, through the simple process of touching and observing, allows us to be in touch with ourselves and to help in the healing process of others. As I treat others, the realization has occurred to me that as I give, I am also receiving. I have found Reiki useful in quelling everything from simple headaches to more chronic conditions.

Nancy Vless

Artist/Teacher

Reiki has really changed my life. I start every day with a full Reiki treatment. When I finish, I feel wonderful, filled with enthusiasm, energy, and joy. Since doing Reiki, I feel less fearful and self-doubting. I have a sense of oneness with the world. I have more confidence in myself. I love myself more and, because of this, feel more loving toward others. I feel that Reiki has deepened my spiritual life and has increased my physical and mental well-being. I recommend Reiki meditation to anyone who wishes to enrich his or her emotional, physical, and spiritual life.

Reiki Training

First Level

Study the history of Reiki, universal principles of healing, and how to give full body treatments to yourself and others. Reiki Master/Teachers will initiate you into Reiki as well as bring to you their own unique philosophy and background in healing. First Level Initiations, also known as attunements, strengthen your direction and vision and make your healing touch more potent.

Second Level

Learn the Reiki sounds and symbols. This ancient language expands your ability to access your knowing mind — your greater mind — directly. The Reiki sounds and symbols are gateways to profound universal qualities. These keys unify time and space (giving us our understanding of absentee healing), align our mental and emotional bodies with spirit, and activate celebrated pathways of directed power. Focus your mind on the sounds and symbols and send healing energy to people long distance (with their permission) and into your own past and future. Learn how to send energy into your affirmations and your purposes.

Second Level Attunements tend to open up the heart and allow you to feel more love, warmth, comfort, and joy for yourself and others. Second Level is recommended for addictive behavior, that is, the habit of focusing outside oneself for satisfaction. Reiki treatments and knowledge give our minds the focus, our bodies the relaxation, and our emotions the love and support to help end addictive behavior.

Reiki Master

Become a Reiki Master and join the power of a group or lineage dedicated to the healing of the planet as well as oneself. Third Level Attunements open up centers of power and action, increasing your ability to manifest directly from spirit. Old patterns and conditioned thoughts fall away as you accept the responsibility of living from a new integrated self. Reiki is a journey, a path of self-mastery.

Third Level Reiki is the knowledge that enables you to do all the initiations/attunements and to teach others. This level is often taught in two parts. In the first section you receive the Third Level Attunement and symbol, and the ability to do a self-attunement. In the second section you receive the knowledge to attune and teach others all the levels of Reiki. The Reiki system is so universal that each teacher has the opportunity to integrate his or her individual background and abilities into the course work.

Reiki Lineage

Between 1973 and 1980, Hawayo Takata initiated and fully trained twenty-three Reiki Masters. The first was Virginia Samdahl and the last Barbara Weber Ray. Ms. Ray received Level One, also referred to as First Degree, from Virginia Samdahl and Levels Two and Three from Ms. Takata. Ms. Ray initiated Maureen O'Toole to Reiki Master with the capability and training to transmit all three Levels and confer Reiki Mastership to others. Barbara and Maureen both initiated Kate Hughson-Law to Third Level Reiki. Maureen transmitted to Kate the capability of conferring Third Degree. In 1987, Kate Hughson-Law imparted Reiki First, Second, and Third Degrees to Marsha Jean Burack, with the capability of conferring First, Second, and Third Degrees to others.

After Ms. Takata's death in 1980, Ms. Ray formed the American International Reiki Association. Phyllis Furumoto, Takata's granddaughter, and other Reiki Masters formed the Reiki Alliance. Many other smaller Reiki groups began as well. In 1985, Kate and several other Reiki Masters developed an independent group called Traditional Reiki Masters. The Reiki Healing Institute was formed in 1989 by Marsha Jean Burack for the purpose of training students and distributing information and materials on Reiki.

Reiki Initiations

My Personal Experience and Psychic Healing

In the beginning, my work was very psychic. I could hear the client's thoughts and ideas in my mind, just as if I were reading a book. I could feel the emotional content of their "dis-ease" and I might comment, "You seem to be going through a lot of indecision lately." I often worked with light coming down through my head and out of my hands. My treatments were very dramatic.

Once I took the Reiki initiations, however, my healing work became simpler and quieter and my hands became warmer. I simply felt expanded in my body, my hands, and my whole being. Long-standing clients felt my work had become more powerful. My questions, my answers, and my energy work addressed the needs of the client or situation very directly, without my actually needing to know the specifics of the problem or dis-ease. It had never been my desire to be a psychic healer or a psychic. I have always wanted simplicity, clarity, and love in my life, and a peaceful, quiet mind. Reiki helped me become more what I wanted to be.

It is my experience that psychic healers or people with trained healing skills move into different modes when they do various types of psychic or energy work. Reiki does not interfere, but is an additional tool. For example, one of my students is a master of Chi Kung (a lengthy study in directing and moving specific kinds of energy). He told me that when he tires of doing Chi Kung, he relaxes and does Reiki. For some people there can even be an opening into new psychic levels of understanding after the Reiki initiations, if there is a natural inclination in that direction. For each person, the initiations have a general gift (see Levels on page 128), as well as a special, unique gift.

Seichim: Reiki-Related Egyptian Healing System

Seichim (pronounced Say keem' or Say sheem') is believed to be an ancient healing system from Egypt going back as far as Atlantis. The hieroglyph Sekhem translates "power of powers" and the symbol is designated by two upraised hands. Patrick Zeigler and Tom Seaman channeled Marat, a 2,500 year-old Sekhem teacher from India who altered and softened the Reiki symbols and gave two new symbols and the ability to initiate students. Kathleen McMasters and Tom Seaman later channeled in additional symbols. It was the intention of the discoverers of this system of living light that people realize that they can access various healing energies through meditating on sacred sounds and symbols. They also encouraged people to create their own symbols and said that many new sound and symbol systems would be appearing at this time.

The applications of Seichim in treatments and absentee healing are identical to Reiki, although each system has its own unique energetic produced by its own attunement process and a different, though related, set of sounds and symbols. I feel Seichim is best taught after Reiki. Reiki expresses as grounded healing energy for this planet. The sounds and symbols of Seichim express as ecstatic, galactic heart energy, whose particular function helps one to overcome obstacles and fears. Where love is, fear disappears.

The Egyptian language has no vowels and so SKHM could be written as Seichim or Sekhem. Sekhem is the Egyptian word for Kundalini or life-force — the serpent power that lies at the base of the spine. Seichim attunements activate this force for healing the heart. Sekhem is ruled by Sekhmet, the lioness Goddess, mother of all the Egyptian Gods. Gods and Goddesses from different cultures are pathways, forms of sacred qualities inherent in man. They are potent reflections of divine powers and abilities latent within each of us. The Goddess Sekhmet is the bestower of all blessings and destroyer of all fears. She is worshipped to this day in the form of statues and amulets.

Seichim is a refined, formless system embodying the most positive energy of this great tradition. Seichim, through a series of attunements and sounds and symbols, moves one to the open and bubbly energy of the free and open heart.

132

Sekhmet Amulet

R. B. D. Images

Photography

Roger B. Daines, CPP.

ABCDDCBA

Reiki and Oriental Painting

My first experience with Oriental painting was with my Zen teacher Sochu San Roshi, a wonderful painter. Our first painting class was to paint the circular form Enzo (on facing page), which represents enlightenment and the universe, ABCDDCBA, the beginning and the end. Class was structured like a meditation. We practiced this circle for twenty minutes without a break, then a walking meditation for ten minutes, and then another twenty minutes of the brush stroke repeated. None of us "westerners" asked for another class! His rendition of this ancient form is superb.

Chinese painting is learned by copying old forms. It is the *chi* or energy of the painting that is important. The beginner learns to paint the four gentlemen Bamboo, Chrysanthemum, Orchid, and Cherry Blossom. By learning the four gentlemen and the ten Chinese numbers, the student knows the most basic strokes.

My Chinese name, Sparkling Star or Crystal-like (see page 139), was given to me by my first Chinese teacher. It is represented by three suns (in the heaven), followed by two fires (dynamic energy moving upward), and one bone stroke (representing the earth plane). The last symbol means jewel. In this pictograph a dash, symbolizing fire, lies sparkling on the earth plane. Ancient writing was based on these powerful, poetic pictographs. When the brush stroke is exact, then there is a corresponding opening in the body and mind.

Reiki is much like this: you learn to focus on ancient sounds and symbols/pictures. Reiki sounds and symbols have the precise property of harmonizing the mind and body so that the deeper life flows through. The real magic of concentrating on symbols and forms is the person's intention to tap deeply into the spiritual energy generating the pictures. The pictures and sounds coupled with our intentions are gateways to profound spiritual qualities. It is the *chi* or energy that counts. In Oriental painting you learn to focus on ancient symbols and forms, and eventually nature, and allow the *chi* or universal energy to flow through you. The painting appears on the page before you. When I do a painting now I draw from life, practice brushstrokes and colors, and then . . . voila! Instant painting!

Paintings by Marsha Burack, a.k.a. Sparkling Star

Three suns (in the heavens)   Two fires (dynamic energy moving upward)   One bone stroke (the earth plane)   Jewel (a dash of fire lies sparkling on the earth plane)

Sparkling Star by Marsha Burack

In Closing

*R*eiki ~ *Healing Yourself & Others, A Photo-Instructional Art Book* is a primer — a basic building block. The concepts and the flow patterns are very simple and, as with all simple truths, profound and substantial. These truths can provide a foundation for a healing practice and any future study. The book's design is elegant, as befits the expression of deeper spiritual life and the dynamic work of bringing love, harmony, and integrity into the cells. *Reiki ~ Healing Yourself & Others* is about self-empowerment. Addressing specific problems is outside the scope of this book and traditional Reiki, although some of the particular uses of Reiki can be found in the testimonials. Often, specific problems are naturally handled by Reiki and the Reiki flow patterns; there are times, however, when other knowledge may speed the healing process for a particular individual. I feel it is usually best to learn a complete system, such as Shiatsu, Jin Shin Jyutsu, Touch for Health, etc. (see reading list). Reiki is a complete system.

If you like this work, I encourage you to continue in Reiki, receive Reiki Initiations, and learn the sounds and symbols and how to apply them in treatments and absentee healing. The knowledge of the Reiki sounds and symbols will enhance not only many kinds of psychotherapeutic techniques but also many other acupressure and laying-on-of-hands systems. I tend to be a structuralist and honor form. Many Reiki teachers use their intuition solely and let it guide them as to where to put their hands. I have not treated in this way; perhaps it is my Zen training. I prefer to use traditional flow patterns and points and vary the time spent at each position. For me, this method enhances a meditative state of mind that allows me to open to complete stillness. I have studied many states of consciousness and I enjoy this form of healing because of its profound meditative and universal qualities. I have seen states of love balance the most complex problems. You will find your own way, or as many Reiki teachers say,

"The Reiki energy will lead you."

The knowledge and understanding of Reiki combined with a dedicated practice will yield a lifetime of gifts.
Reiki is a promise — a promise of growth and fulfillment.

About the Author

Marsha Burack showed an interest in spiritual development at the age of thirteen when she began studying philosophies and religions of all kinds. When she was twenty, she began Zen meditation, which she continues to practice in her daily life. Marsha graduated with honors from the University of California at Berkeley in art and anthropology — with a special interest in healing and healers. After graduation, she lived in England for seven years, concentrating on her family, art, and English culture.

Returning to the United States, Marsha immersed herself in studying, teaching yoga, and her artwork. She then suffered an injury, which led her to pursue an interest in various healing techniques. The rewarding results that began on a personal level grew into a desire to help and work with others. Since 1978, Marsha has worked as a body worker/healer, continually adding to training credentials that include certification in Jin Shin Jyutsu, Bach Flowers, Touch for Health, Rebirthing, Reiki, and Seichim. For ten years, she practiced Integral Consciousness Training, which enables one to shift one's usual mental and emotional state of mind to a more refined level of consciousness. This training provided a good background for becoming a Reiki teacher. After Marsha became a Traditional Reiki Master in 1987, she began teaching Reiki and developing unique, powerful teaching tools. Marsha brings to her teaching a flexible, practical approach that furthers each individual's progress with clarity and sensitivity.

Outside of her healing profession, Marsha's work as an artist is a major pursuit. Chinese brush painting, watercolors, and oils are her specialties. The paintings in this book are all examples of her work. In addition, Marsha has raised two sons in a very conscientious manner. The boys are now in their twenties and are already exhibiting a marked influence from growing up in an atmosphere filled with creativity and healing.

This book was designed by Marsha as a comprehensive guide to those interested in Reiki and hands-on healing. With her incredible dedication to healing, Marsha Burack can serve as an inspiration to each of us that improving our health is within our reach.

DeeAna Alexandria

Suggested Reading List

The Healer's Hand Book. Georgina Regan and Debbie Shapiro.
Rockport, MA: Element, Inc., 1991.

Relax! with Self-Therap/ease. Bonnie Pendleton and Betty Mehling.
P.O. Box 14, Calabasas, CA 91302: California Publications, 1976.

Your Healing Hands: The Polarity Experience. Richard Gordon.
Oakland, CA: Wingbow Press, 1978.

Acupressure Way of Health: Jin Shin Do. Iona Teeguarden.
Tokyo, Japan: Japan Publications, Inc., 1978.

Acupuncture without Needles. J.V. Cerney, A.B., D.M., P.P.M.
USA: D.C. Parker Publishing, Inc., 1983.

Japanese Finger-Pressure Therapy SHIATSU. Tokujiro Namikoshi.
Tokyo, Japan: Japan Publications, Inc., 1969.

Helping Yourself with Foot Reflexology. Mildred Carter.
West Nyack, NY: Parker Publishing, 1978.

Body Reflexology. Mildred Carter. West Nyack, NY:
Parker Publishing, 1983.

Touch for Health: A New Approach to Restoring Our Natural Energies, 3d rev. ed. John F. Thie D.C. 1200 N. Lake Ave., Pasadena CA: T.H. Enterprises, 1987.

Light Emerging: The Journey of Personal Healing. Barbara Ann Brennan. New York: Bantam Books, 1993.

The Anatomy Coloring Book. Wynn Kapit and Lawrence M. Elson. New York: HarperCollins College Publishers, 1993.

The Bach Flower Remedies. Edward Bach. New Canaan, CT: M.D. Keats Publishing, Inc., 1952.

The Body Electric: Electromagnetism and the Foundation of Life. Robert Becker, M.D., and Gary Selden. NY: Morrow, 1985.

Energy Matter and Form. Christopher Hills, gen. ed. Boulder Creek, CA: University of the Trees Press, 1977.

Wheels of Life: A User's Guide to the Chakra System. Anodea Judith. St. Paul, MN: Llewellyn Publications, 1989.

The Chakras. C.W. Leadbeater. Wheaton, IL: Theosophical Publishing House, 1987.

The Mystic Spiral. Jill Purce. New York: Thames and Hudson, Inc., 1990.

The Rainbow Bridge. Two Disciples. P.O. Box 929, Danville, CA 94526: Rainbow Bridge Productions, 1982.

Prayers of the Cosmos: Meditations on the Aramaic Words of Jesus. Neil Douglas-Klotz, trans. San Francisco, CA: HarperCollins Publishers, 1990.

It Is ALL Right. Isabel M. Hickey. 103 Goldencrest Ave., Waltham, MA 02154: New Pathways, 1990.

Kofutu Touch Healing. Frank Homan and Verna Kragnes. 3907 Tonkawood Rd., Minnetonka, MN 55345: Kofutu Books, 1986.

Reiki Books

Reiki: Hawayo Takata's Story. Helen J. Haberly. P.O. Box 557, Garrett Park, MD, 20896: Archedigm Publications, 1990.

The "Reiki" Factor in the Radiance Technique, exp. ed. Barbara Ray. Petersburg, FL: Radiance Associates, 1985.

Reiki: Universal Life Energy. Bodo J. Baginski and Shalila Sharamon. Mendocino, CA: Life Rhythm, 1988.

Empowerment through Reiki. Paula Horan. Wilmot, WI: Lotus Light Publications, 1990.

Reiki in Everyday Living. Earlene Gleisner. Laytonville, CA: White Feather Press, 1992.

Also of Interest

Healers and the Healing Process. George W. Meek. Wheaton, IL: Theosophical Publishing House, 1977.

Rio Tigre and Beyond: The Amazon Jungle Medicine of Manuel Cordova. Bruce Lamb. Berkeley, CA: North Atlantic Books, 1985.

The Man Who Tapped the Secrets of the Universe. Glenn Clark. Swannanoa, Waynesboro, VA: University of Science and Philosophy, 1980.

The Celestine Prophecy: An Adventure. James Redfield. New York, NY: Warner Books, Inc., 1993.

Mutant Message: Down Under. Marlo Morgan. P.O. Box 100, Lees Summit, MO, 64063: M M Company, 1991.

Behaving As If the God in All Life Mattered: *A New Age Ecology.* Machaelle Small Wright. P.O. Box 3603, Warrenton, VA 22186: Perelandra, Ltd., 1987.

Energy-Enhancing Sources

The Secret of the Creative Vacuum: Man and the Energy Dance. John Davidson. Great Britain: C.W. Daniel Company, Ltd., 1989.

Biocircuits: Amazing New Tools for Energy Health. Leslie and Terry Patten. Tiburon, CA: H. J. Kramer, Inc., 1988.

The Ion Effect: *How Air Electricity Rules Your Life and Health.* Fred Soyka. New York, NY: E.P. Dutton & Co., Inc., 1978.

Reverse Aging: Scientific Health Methods Easier and More Effective than Diet and Exercise. Sang Whang. Englewood Cliff, NJ: Siloam Enterprise, Inc., 1990. Natural Plus Plus 813-447-2344.

Elixir of the Ageless: *You Are What You Drink.* Dr. Patrick Flanagan. 22 S. San Francisco St., Flagstaff, AZ 86001: Vortex Press, 1986.

Suggested Music

DNA Music, Molecular Meditation. Riley McLaughlin. Walnut Creek, CA: Science and the Arts, 1985.

Reiki ~ Healing Yourself . . . Music Only. Kristopher Witty. Encinitas, CA: Reiki Healing Institute, 1990.

Products and Services

Reiki ~ Healing Yourself **Audiocassetes**

101 **Treatment Tape** — Inspirational words and angelic music, designed to open your heart, will guide you through a full hands-on body treatment (Head Flow Treatment on pages 28-59).

102 **Treatment Tape** — The voice is intensified for the hearing impaired.

103 **Music Only Tape** — Treat yourself at your own rate to the atmospheric music of Kristopher Witty. The music will remind your body/mind of the healing words on the **Treatment Tape**.

104 **Two Tape Set** — Contains **Treatment and Music Only Tapes**, plus booklet, in a beautiful gift album.

The **Reiki Healing Institute** in Encinitas, CA offers classes taught by Marsha Burack, in **Reiki and/or Seichim**:

Level I — Receive Attunements and learn to treat others and yourself. Learn the history of **Reiki**.

Level II — Receive the Second Level Attunement. Learn the Sounds and Symbols and amplify your **Reiki** treatments. Learn absentee healing and techniques to heal your past and enhance your future.

Level III — Master/Teacher Training. Receive the Third Level Attunement and Sound and Symbol. Learn to self-initiate, and then to teach and initiate others into **Reiki** (see pages 4, 128, 129).

Reiki Healing Institute Referral System:

Students — obtain information on teachers in your area or how to develop a seminar in your area.

Teachers — join the referral system and we will network students to you.

For information please write the **Reiki Healing Institute** • 449 Santa Fe Drive, # 303 • Encinitas, CA 92024.
Fax (619) 436-6875 • Phone 760-436-1865 • e-mail address empower@webtv.net
You many order directly at http://www.pblsh.com/Healthworks/reiki.html (or bookorder.html).

Every day is a good day, every day is a sacred day, and every place is a sacred place.

Order Form

Please photocopy this page and fill in the following information:

Reiki - Healing Yourself **Audiocassette Tapes:**

Treatment Tape .... Qty ___ at $12.95 per tape _____

Voice-Intensified .... Qty ___ at $12.95 per tape _____

Music Only .... Qty ___ at $ 9.95 per tape _____

Treatment & Music Only Tapes packaged in a

    Gift Album .... Qty ___ at $22.50 per set _____

Additional copies of *Reiki ~ Healing Yourself & Others,*
A Photo-Instructional Art Book ....Qty ___ at $24.95 per book _____

Art Book and Treatment Tape .... Qty ___ at $34.95 per set _____

Art Book and Gift Album .... Qty ___ at $42.50 per set _____

                                       SUBTOTAL _____

California Residents, add applicable Sales Tax _____

S&H - Book $5, additional Bks $3 ea., Tape $3.50, additional Tapes $1.50 ea.
Book and Tape $6, Book and Gift Album $6, Additional Sets $4 _____

                                         TOTAL _____

Check box for: ❏ **Reiki/Seichim Classes by Marsha Burack or staff**

❏ **Reiki and/or Seichim Levels I and II**   ❏ **Level III — Master Training**

❏ Referral • Teachers wanting students   ❏ Students wanting teachers

Send check, money order, or credit card information to: **Reiki Healing Institute**
449 Santa Fe Drive, # 303 • Encinitas, CA 92024 • Call 760-436-1865 • Fax 760-436-6875 • Order directly at http://www.pblsh.com/Healthworks/reiki.html

Name_____ Phone (_____) _____

Address_____

City, State, Zip_____

May REIKI renew your soul,
ease your mind, free your spirit
& bring joy to your heart.